LEARN TO
Quilt With Fat Quarters

Posy Cozy & Coasters, page 64

www.companyscoming.com
visit our website

A Stitch in Time Tote, page 102

Learn to Quilt With Fat Quarters

Copyright © Company's Coming Publishing Limited

First Printing April 2011

Library and Archives Canada Cataloguing in Publication
Learn to quilt with fat quarters.
(Workshop series)
Includes index.
ISBN 978-1-897477-48-9
1.Quilting. 2. Quilting--Patterns.
I. Series: Workshop series (Edmonton, Alta.)
TT835.L43 2010   746.46   C2010-903666-2

Published by
Company's Coming Publishing Limited
2311-96 Street
Edmonton, Alberta, Canada T6N 1G3
Tel: 780-450-6223 Fax: 780-450-1857
www.companyscoming.com

Company's Coming is a registered trademark owned by Company's Coming Publishing Limited

Printed in China

The Company's Coming Story

Jean Paré grew up with an understanding that family, friends and home cooking are the key ingredients for a good life. A mother of four, Jean worked as a professional caterer for 18 years, operating out of her home kitchen. During that time, she came to appreciate quick and easy recipes that call for everyday ingredients. In answer to mounting requests for her recipes, Company's Coming cookbooks were born, and Jean moved on to a new chapter in her career.

Company's Coming founder Jean Paré

In the beginning, Jean worked from a spare bedroom in her home, located in the small prairie town of Vermilion, Alberta, Canada. The first Company's Coming cookbook, *150 Delicious Squares*, was an immediate bestseller. Today, with well over 150 titles in print, Company's Coming has earned the distinction of publishing Canada's most popular cookbooks. The company continues to gain new supporters by adhering to Jean's "Golden Rule of Cooking"—Never share a recipe you wouldn't use yourself. It's an approach that has worked—millions of times over!

Company's Coming cookbooks are distributed throughout Canada, the United States, Australia and other international English-language markets. French and Spanish language editions have also been published. Sales to date have surpassed 25 million copies with no end in sight. Familiar and trusted in home kitchens around the world, Company's Coming cookbooks are highly regarded both as kitchen workbooks and as family heirlooms.

Just as Company's Coming continues to promote the tradition of home cooking, the same is now true with crafting. Like good cooking, great craft results depend upon easy-to-follow instructions, readily available materials and enticing photographs of the finished products. Also like cooking, crafting is meant to be enjoyed in the home or cottage. Company's Coming Crafts, then, is a natural extension from the kitchen into the family room or den.

Because Company's Coming operates a test kitchen and not a craft shop, we've partnered with a major North American craft content publisher to assemble a variety of craft compilations exclusively for us. Our editors have been involved every step of the way. You can see the excellent results for yourself in the book you're holding.

Company's Coming Crafts are for everyone—whether you're a beginner or a seasoned pro. What better gift could you offer than something you've made yourself? In these hectic days, people still enjoy crafting parties; they bring family and friends together in the same way a good meal does. Company's Coming is proud to support crafters with this new creative book series.

We hope you enjoy these easy-to-follow, informative and colourful books, and that they inspire your creativity. So, don't delay—get crafty!

TABLE OF CONTENTS

Foreword 7 • Quilt-Making Basics 8

Hugs & Kisses Baby Blanket, page 18

Welcoming Baby

Fill every stitch with love as you create a special gift to welcome a new little one into your life.

Hugs & Kisses Baby Blanket 18
Sweet Baby Quilt 22
Baby Block Play Mat 25
Baby Blocks With Love 28
Stitched With Love Quilt & Tote 32
Baby Bibs Twins 38
Down on the Farm Gift Set 44

Dress Your Table

Add zip and colour to any room with one of these fun and easy runners stitched from fat quarters.

Summer Delight Runner 49
Pink & Green Squared 52
Sunflower Sensation 56
Cherry Pickin' 59
Posy Cozy & Coasters 64
Floral Silhouettes 69

Stitched With Love Quilt & Tote, page 32

Cherry Pickin', page 59

Sunflower Sensation, page 56

TABLE OF CONTENTS

Index 124 • General Information 126

Simple Throws & Quilts

Stitch these fabulous quilts and throws featuring stripes, blooming flowers and bright colours.

Tumbling Stripes Throw...................... 74
Garden Patch Quilt 76
Sunny Days... 80
Pretty Maids... 84
Windmill Twin Quilt............................. 89
Maple Leaf Ragtime 92
Warm & Cozy Flannel Throw........... 96

Quick-to-Stitch Surprises

When time is of the essence, turn the pages in this chapter to find a perfect quilted item to make in a hurry.

Pretty & Pieced..................................... 99
A Stitch in Time Tote......................... 102
Appliquéd Towel Trio......................... 105
Patchwork Backpack 108
Sit With Me & Have Some Tea...... 112
Pretty & Pink....................................... 116
Little Scrappy Pincushions 119

Little Scrappy Pincushions, page 119

Pretty Maids, page 84

Sit With Me & Have Some Tea, page 112

Windmill Twin Quilt, page 89

Make it yourself!

COMPANY'S COMING
CRAFT WORKSHOP BOOKS

LEARN TO *Sew for the Table*

LEARN TO *Knit for Baby*

Kids LEARN TO *Knit, Quilt & Crochet*

27 easy-to-make projects

Step-by-step instructions

Colour photos of every project

LEARN TO *Knit in the Round*

LEARN TO *Make Cards With Photos*

LEARN TO *Quilt With Panels*

Learn To *Knit Socks*

Learn To *Crochet in a Day*

LEARN TO *Craft With Paper*

LEARN TO *Bead Jewellery*

Learn To *Bead Earrings*

89 easy-to-make projects
Step-by-step instructions
Colour photos of every project

CRAFT WORKSHOP SERIES

Get a craft class in a book! General instructions teach basic skills or how to apply them in a new way. Easy-to-follow steps, diagrams and photos make projects simple.

Whether paper crafting, knitting, crocheting, beading, sewing or quilting—find beautiful, fun designs you can make yourself.

For a complete listing of Company's Coming cookbooks and craft books, check out
www.companyscoming.com

FOREWORD

Isn't it fun to buy fat quarters! One of the first things we look for in a quilt shop is fat quarters. Shops are full of creative displays of fat quarters in a variety of fabrics and a rainbow of colours. In the same way, there are many creative ways to use fat quarters. This book is full of great designs that will inspire you to use fat quarters for your next quilting project.

Creating a quilt for a new baby is a time-honoured tradition women enjoy with each new generation. For many quilters, a baby quilt is the first quilt they make. Stitching a baby quilt using fat quarters is both fun and easy. What better way to say, "I love you" to a new little one than with a soft, cuddly quilt, a handy tote or even a patchwork bib.

Fat quarters are perfect for creating table runners. Runners are small, and most of the time you can make a runner in one evening with just a few fat quarters. The runners in this chapter include simple appliqué, yo-yos, embroidery and bright colours. We've even included a cute cozy and coaster set to use for a special afternoon tea around your table.

Our collection would not be complete without some simple, yet fabulous, throws and quilts. Whether you need a twin-size quilt for a coed going off to college or a lap-size quilt for an aging parent, you'll find an assortment of designs in this chapter. Pick your favourite colours in coordinating fat quarters to make a great quilt for your home or to give as a gift.

If time is at a premium, the surprise items in our last chapter are perfect for you. Choose from an array of projects, including a handy backpack, a pieced tote and some pretty book covers. You can even use some of your leftover fat quarters to create some cute pincushions.

All the projects in this book are either beginner or easy—perfect for someone at either skill level. Full-page colour photos and clearly written instructions with illustrations make it easy to create a fabulous item. It's time to get started quilting with fat quarters!

Garden Patch Quilt, page 76

QUILT-MAKING BASICS

Materials & Supplies

Fat-Quarter Fabrics

Fat quarters are fabric yardage cut half the fabric width by half a yard—in most fabrics this size is 22" x 18". For some projects, this size works better than a regular quarter-yard of fabric that would be 9" by the width of the fabric, usually 42"–45".

Some projects require pieces larger than 9" for appliqué shapes or corner triangles. These larger shapes cannot be cut from a quarter-yard of fabric, but can be cut from fat quarters.

Most fabric stores will not custom-cut fat quarters, but they do sell them. They choose which fabrics they want to cut up for this purpose. In some stores, just one fat quarter is available, while in other stores coordinated sets of fabric are selected and bundled in an attractive way to show off the colours. These bundles are hard to resist.

If you like to have lots of different fabrics available whenever you start to sew, collect fat quarters in a variety of colours and prints, and get ready to have some fun.

Thread

For most piecing, good-quality cotton or cotton-covered polyester is the thread of choice. Inexpensive polyester threads are not recommended because they can cut the fibres of cotton fabrics.

Choose a colour thread that will match or blend with the fabrics in your quilt. For projects pieced with dark- or light-coloured fabrics, choose a neutral thread colour, such as a medium grey, as a compromise between colours. Test by pulling a sample seam.

Batting

Batting is the material used to give a quilt loft or thickness. It also adds warmth.

Some qualities to look for in batting are drapeability, resistance to fibre migration, loft and softness.

Tools & Equipment

There are few truly essential tools and little equipment required for quilt making. Basics include needles (hand-sewing and betweens), pins (long, thin, sharp pins are best), sharp scissors or shears, a thimble, template materials (plastic or cardboard), marking tools (chalk marker, water-erasable pen and a No. 2 pencil, are a few) and a quilting frame or hoop. For piecing and/or quilting by machine, add a sewing machine to the list.

Other sewing basics such as a seam ripper, pincushion, measuring tape and an iron are also necessary. For making strip-pieced quilts, a rotary cutter, rotary cutting mat and specialty rulers are essential.

Construction Methods

Traditional Templates

There are two types—templates that include a ¼" seam allowance and those that don't.

Choose the template material and the pattern. Transfer the pattern shapes to the template material with a sharp No. 2 pencil. Write the pattern name, piece letter or number, grain line and number to cut for one block or whole quilt on each piece as shown in Figure 1.

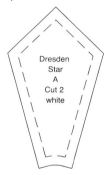

Figure 1

Some patterns require a reversed piece (Figure 2). These patterns are labelled with an R after the piece letter; for example, B and BR. To reverse a template, first cut it with the labelled side up and then with the labelled side down. Or, place two layers of fabric with right sides together and cut two pieces at once; one will be reversed.

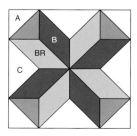

Figure 2

Machine-Piecing

If making templates, include the ¼" seam allowance on the template for machine-piecing. Place template on the wrong side of the fabric as for hand-piecing, except butt pieces against one another when tracing.

Set machine on 2.5 or 12–15 stitches per 1". Join pieces as for hand-piecing, beginning and ending sewing at the end of the fabric patch. No backstitching is necessary when machine-stitching.

Quick-Cutting

Templates can be completely eliminated when using a rotary cutter with a plastic ruler and mat to cut fabric strips.

Always cut away from your body, holding the ruler firmly with the non-cutting hand.

Cutting Strips

Iron fabric to remove wrinkles. Fold in half lengthwise, bringing selvages together. Fold in half again (Figure 3). Be sure there aren't any wrinkles in the fabric.

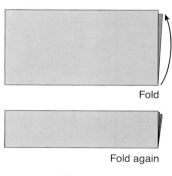

Fold

Fold again

Figure 3

Square up fabric first. Place folded fabric on cutting mat with the fabric length on the right or left for left-handed cutters (Figure 4). Line up fold of fabric along one of the mat grid lines.

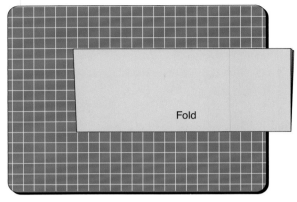

Right-handed

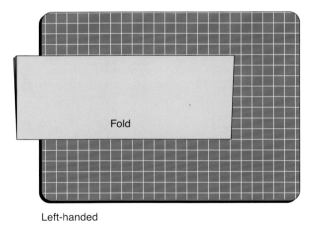

Left-handed

Figure 4

Place acrylic ruler near cut edge, with ruler markings even with mat grid. Hold ruler firmly with left hand (right hand for left-handers), with small finger off the mat to provide extra stability. Hold rotary cutter with blade against ruler and cut away from you in one motion (Figure 5).

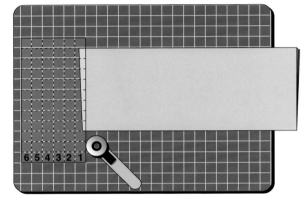

Right-handed

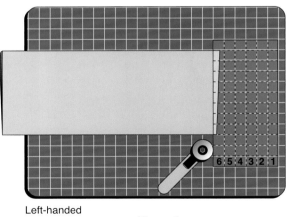

Left-handed

Figure 5

Place ruler with appropriate width line along cut edge of fabric and cut strip (Figure 6). Continue cutting the number of strips needed for your project.

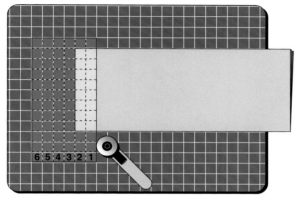

Right-handed

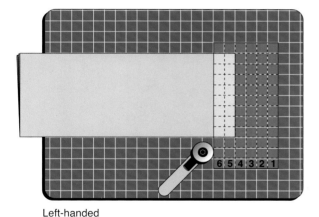

Left-handed

Figure 6

Note: After cutting a few strips, check to make sure your fabric is squared up and re-square if necessary. If you don't, your strips may have a "v" in the centre (Figure 7), causing inaccurate piecing.

Figure 7

Quick-Piecing Method

Lay pieces to be joined under the presser foot of the sewing machine right sides together. Sew an exact ¼" seam allowance to the end of the piece; place another unit right next to the first one and continue sewing, adding a piece after every stitched piece, until all of the pieces are used up (Figure 8).

Figure 8

When sewing is finished, cut the threads that join the pieces apart. Press seam toward the darker fabric.

Appliqué

Making Templates

The appliqué designs given in this book are shown as full-size drawings. The drawings show dotted lines to indicate where one piece overlaps another. Other marks indicate placement of embroidery stitches for decorative purposes such as eyes, lips, flowers, etc.

Before the actual appliqué process begins, cut the background block.

Transfer the design to a large piece of tracing paper. Using a light box, transfer design to fabric background.

If you don't have a light box, tape the pattern on a window; centre the background block on top and tape in place. Trace the design onto the background block with a water-erasable marker, or light lead or chalk pencil. This drawing will mark exactly where the fabric pieces should be placed on the background block.

Hand Appliqué

Traditional hand appliqué uses a template made from the desired finished shape without seam allowance added.

After fabric is prepared, trace the desired shape onto the right side of the fabric with a water-erasable marker, or light lead or chalk pencil. Leave at least ½" between design motifs when tracing to allow for the seam allowance when cutting out the shapes.

When the desired number of shapes needed has been drawn on the fabric pieces, cut out shapes, leaving ⅛"–¼" all around drawn line for turning under.

Turn the shape's edges over on the drawn or stitched line. When turning in concave curves, clip to seams, and baste the seam allowance over as shown in Figure 9.

Figure 9

For hand appliqué, position the fabric shapes on the background block and pin or baste them in place. Using a blind stitch or appliqué stitch, sew pieces in place with matching thread and small stitches. Start with background pieces first and work up to foreground pieces.

Machine Appliqué

There are several products available to help make the machine-appliqué process easier and faster.

Fusible transfer web is a commercial product similar to iron-on interfacings except it has two sticky sides. It is used to adhere appliqué shapes to the background with heat. Paper is adhered to one side of the web.

To use, reverse pattern and draw shapes onto the paper side of the web; cut, leaving a margin around each shape. Place on the wrong side of the chosen fabric; fuse in place, referring to the manufacturer's instructions. Cut out shapes on the drawn line. Peel off the paper and fuse in place on the background fabric. Transfer any detail lines to the fabric shapes.

Putting It All Together

Finishing the Top

Settings

Most quilts are made by sewing individual blocks together in rows that, when joined, create a design.

Plain blocks can be alternated with pieced or appliquéd blocks in a straight set (Figure 1).

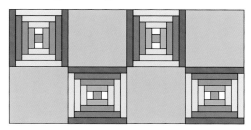

Figure 1

Adding Borders

Borders are an integral part of the quilt and should complement the colours and designs used in the quilt centre.

If fabric strips are added for borders, they may be mitred (Figure 2) or butted (Figure 3) at the corners. To determine the size for butted border strips, measure across the centre of the completed quilt top from one side raw edge to the other side raw edge. This measurement will include a ¼" seam allowance.

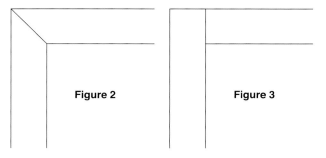

Figure 2   **Figure 3**

Cut two border strips that length by the chosen width of the border. Sew these strips to the top and bottom of the pieced centre, referring to Figure 4. Press the seam allowance toward the border strips.

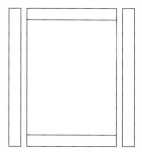

Figure 4

Measure across the completed quilt top at the centre, from top raw edge to bottom raw edge, including the two border strips already added. Cut two border strips that length by the chosen width of the border. Sew a strip to each of the two remaining sides as shown in Figure 4. Press the seams toward the border strips.

To make mitred corners, measure the quilt as before. Add twice the finished width of the border, to allow for mitring, plus ½" for seam allowances to the vertical quilt measurement to determine the length of side border strips. Repeat for horizontal or top and bottom sides. Sew on each strip, stopping stitching ¼" from corner (Figure 5), leaving the remainder of the strip dangling.

Figure 5

Press corners at a 45-degree angle to form a crease (Figure 6). Stitch from the inside quilt corner to the outside on the creased line. Trim excess away after stitching and press mitred seams open (Figure 7).

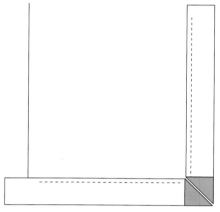

Figure 6

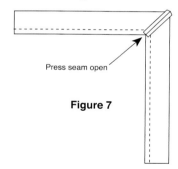

Press seam open

Figure 7

Getting Ready to Quilt

Choosing a Quilting Design

There are several types of quilting designs, some of which may not have to be marked. The easiest of the unmarked designs is in-the-ditch quilting. Here, the quilting stitches are placed in the valley created by the seams joining two pieces together or next to the edge of an appliqué design (Figure 8).

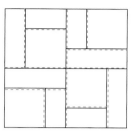

Figure 8

Outline quilting ¼" or more away from seams or appliqué shapes is another no-mark alternative (Figure 9) that prevents having to sew through the layers made by seams, thus making stitching easier.

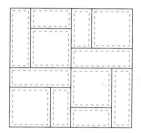

Figure 9

Meander or free-motion quilting by machine fills in open spaces and doesn't require marking. It is fun and easy to stitch as shown in Figure 10.

Figure 10

Marking the Top for Quilting

If you choose a fancy or all-over design for quilting, you will need to transfer the design to your quilt top before layering with the backing and batting. You may use a sharp, medium-lead or silver pencil on light background fabrics. Test the pencil marks to guarantee that they will wash out of your quilt top when quilting is complete; or be sure your quilting stitches cover the pencil marks. Mechanical pencils with very fine points may be used successfully to mark quilts.

Preparing the Quilt Backing

A backing is generally cut at least 4" larger than the quilt top or 2" larger on all sides. For a 64" x 78" finished quilt, the backing would need to be at least 68" x 82".

To avoid having the seam across the centre of the quilt backing, cut or tear one of the right-length pieces in half and sew half to each side of the second piece as shown in Figure 11.

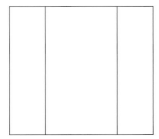

Figure 11

Layering the Quilt Sandwich

Open the batting several days before you need it, to help flatten the creases caused from its being folded up in the bag for so long. Iron the backing piece.

To hold the quilt layers together for quilting, baste by hand or use safety pins. If basting by hand, thread a long thin needle with a long piece of unknotted white or off-white thread. Starting in the centre and leaving a long tail, make 4"–6" stitches toward the outside edge of the quilt top, smoothing as you baste. Start at the centre again and work toward the outside as shown in Figure 12.

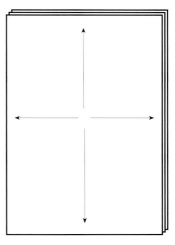

Figure 12

If quilting by machine, you may prefer to use safety pins for holding your fabric sandwich together. Start in the centre of the quilt and pin to the outside, leaving pins open until all are placed. When you are satisfied that all layers are smooth, close the pins.

Quilting

Hand Quilting

To begin, thread a sharp, between needle with an 18" piece of quilting thread. Tie a small knot in the end of the thread. Position the needle about ½" to 1" away from the starting point on quilt top. Sink the needle through the top into the batting layer but not through the backing. Pull the needle up at the starting point of the quilting design. Pull the needle and thread until the knot sinks through the top into the batting (Figure 13).

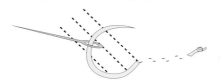

Figure 13

Take small, even running stitches along the marked quilting line. Keep one hand positioned underneath to feel the needle go all the way through to the backing.

When you have nearly run out of thread, wind the thread around the needle several times to make a small knot and pull it close to the fabric. Insert the needle into the fabric on the quilting line and come out with the needle ½" to 1" away, pulling the knot into the fabric layers the same as when you started. Pull and cut thread close to fabric. The end should disappear inside after cutting. Some quilters prefer to take a backstitch with a loop through it for a knot to end.

Machine Quilting

Successful machine quilting requires practice and a good relationship with your sewing machine.

Prepare the quilt for machine quilting in the same way as for hand quilting. Use safety pins to hold the layers together.

Set the machine on a longer stitch length (3.0 or 8–10 stitches per 1") and loosen the amount of pressure on the presser foot. If using marked quilting designs, stitch along the quilting line. An even-feed or walking foot helps to eliminate tucks and puckering by feeding the upper and lower layers through the machine evenly. Special machine-quilting needles work best to penetrate the three layers in your quilt.

Finishing the Edges

To prepare the quilt for the addition of the binding, trim the batting and backing layers flush with the top of the quilt. Using a walking-foot attachment (sometimes called an even-feed foot attachment), machine-baste the three layers together all around, approximately ⅛" from the cut edge.

The materials listed for each quilt often include a number of yards of self-made or purchased binding. The advantage to self-made binding is that you can use fabrics from your quilt to coordinate colours.

Double-fold, straight-grain binding is used on projects with right-angle corners. To make this binding, cut 2¼"-wide strips of fabric across the width or down the length of the fabric totalling the perimeter of the quilt plus 10". The strips are joined, as shown in Figure 14, and pressed in half wrong sides together along the length, using an iron on a cotton setting with no steam.

Figure 14

Lining up the raw edges, place the binding on the top of the quilt and begin sewing (again using the walking foot) approximately 6" from the beginning of the binding strip. Stop sewing ¼" from the first corner, leave the needle in the quilt, turn and sew diagonally to the corner as shown in Figure 15.

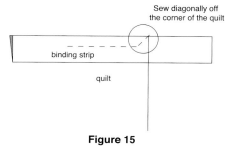

Sew diagonally off
the corner of the quilt

binding strip

quilt

Figure 15

Fold the binding at a 45-degree angle up and away from the quilt as shown in Figure 16 and back down flush with the raw edges. Starting at the top raw edge of the quilt, begin sewing the next side as shown in Figure 17. Repeat at the next three corners.

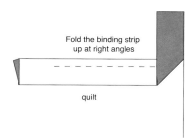

Fold the binding strip
up at right angles

quilt

Figure 16

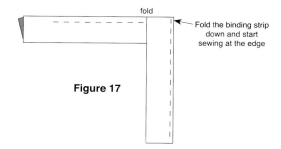

fold

Fold the binding strip
down and start
sewing at the edge

Figure 17

As you approach the beginning of the binding strip, stop stitching and overlap the binding ½" from the edge; trim. Join the two ends with a ¼" seam allowance and press the seam open. Reposition the joined binding along the edge of the quilt and resume stitching to the beginning.

To finish, bring the folded edge of the binding over the raw edges, and blind stitch the binding in place over the machine-stitching line on the back side. Hand-mitre the corners on the back as shown in Figure 18.

Figure 18

HUGS & KISSES BABY BLANKET

The round corner tabs make for easy grabbing as this little blanket becomes a constant companion.

Design | Lisa Swenson Ruble

Project Specifications

Skill Level: Beginner
Quilt Size: 22½" x 22½", excluding corner tabs

Materials

1 fat quarter each turquoise mini print, blue dot, lime mini print and yellow dot
2 fat quarters large dot
27" x 27" square coordinating solid for backing
Batting 27" x 27" and 18" x 18"

Cutting

Cut four 3" x 22" strips from turquoise mini print fat quarter. Subcut into (25) 3" squares.

Cut three 3" x 22" strips from blue dot fat quarter. Subcut into (20) 3" squares.

From lime mini print fat quarter, cut two 3⅜" x 22" strips and subcut into eight 3⅜" squares; cut three 3" x 22" strips and subcut into (16) 3" squares.

From yellow dot fat quarter, cut two 3⅜" x 22" strips and subcut into eight 3⅜" squares; cut one 3" x 22" strip and subcut into four 3" squares.

Prepare template for A using pattern given; cut eight A pieces from large dot fat quarters.

Prepare template for B using pattern given; cut four B pieces from 18" x 18" batting.

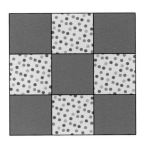 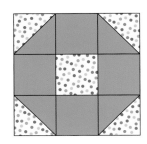

X Block
7½" x 7½" Block
Make 5

O Block
7½" x 7½" Block
Make 4

Completing the Blocks

Referring to X Block diagram, sew blue dot and turquoise squares together to make five pieced blocks.

On the wrong side of 3⅜" yellow dot squares, draw diagonal lines from corner to corner (Figure 1).

Figure 1

Sew each yellow dot square to a lime mini print square, sewing ¼" on each side of the diagonal line (Figure 2).

Figure 2

Hugs & Kisses Baby Blanket

Cut each on the diagonal line to make 16 triangle units (Figure 3). Referring to O Block diagram (see page 18), sew 3" yellow-dot squares, 3" lime mini print squares, and triangle units together to make four pieced blocks.

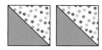

Figure 3

Completing the Quilt

Using the photo as a guide, sew pieced blocks together as shown.

Pair two large dot circles right sides together and sew around edge, leaving an opening as indicated on template. Turn right side out. Press flat. Insert batting circle. Pin in place and quilt as desired. *Note: Opening will be covered by quilt corners.* Repeat to make a total of four circles.

Layer quilt backing and quilt top right sides together on top of batting. Pin layers together. Sew around outer edge, leaving approximately 3" at each corner for inserting quilted circles.

Trim excess backing and batting. Turn right side out through corner opening. Press under seam allowances at corner openings.

Sandwich quilted circles between layers and pin in place. Topstitch edges of quilt ¼" from edge. Hand- or machine-quilt pieced blocks as desired. ■

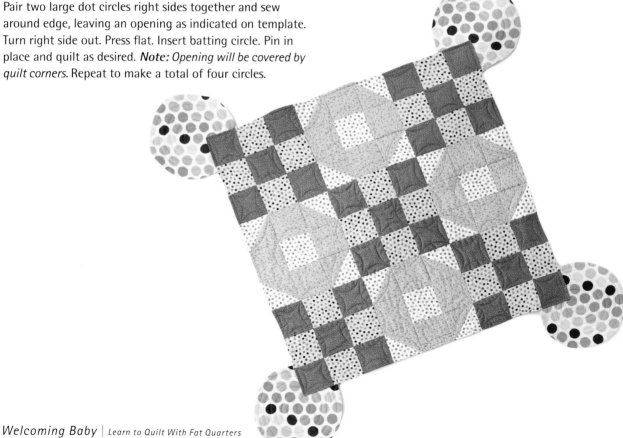

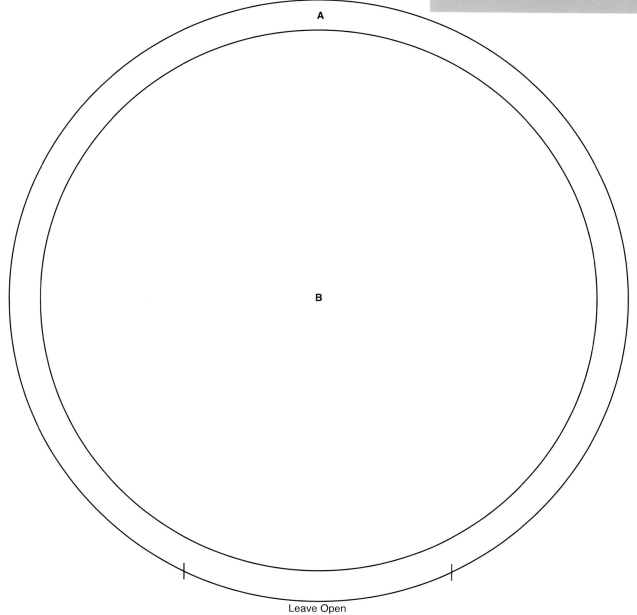

A

B

Leave Open

Hugs & Kisses Baby Blanket
Template
Actual Size

SWEET BABY QUILT

This pretty pastel quilt for a special baby is a thoughtful gift for the new mother and child.

Design | Connie Kauffman

Project Specifications
Skill Level: Beginner
Quilt Size: 32" x 37"

Materials
1 fat quarter cotton fabric each light-baby print, pink print, violet print, yellow print and pastel blue print
¾ yard light yellow cotton print,
1⅛ yards pastel pink cotton print, for backing
Batting 38" x 43"
Multicoloured cotton thread

Cutting
From five cotton fat quarters, cut four 5½" squares from each.

Cut five 2½" x 5½" rectangles each from four fat quarters, and four 2½" x 5½" rectangles from the remaining fat quarter.

From ¾ yard light yellow print, cut two 2½" x 24½" strips for inner top and bottom borders, two 2½" x 25½" strips for inner side borders, two 2½" x 32½" strips for outer top and bottom borders, two 2½" x 33½" strips for outside borders, and four 2" strips the width of the fabric for binding.

Completing the Quilt
Refer to Placement Diagram to sew 5½" x 5½" blocks into five rows of four blocks each. Sew rows together to make centre of quilt.

Sew inner side borders to sides of pieced blocks. Sew inner top and bottom borders across top and bottom.

Sew short edges of 2½" x 5½" rectangles to make a top, a bottom and two side-pieced border strips of six rectangles each.

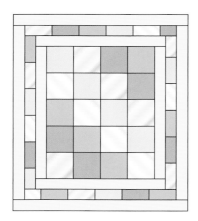

Sweet Baby Quilt
Placement Diagram
32" x 37"

Sweet Baby Quilt

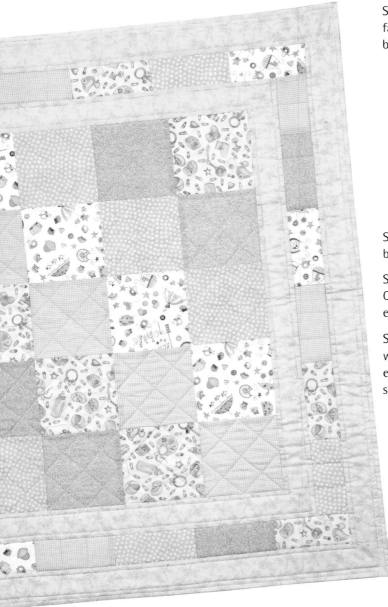

Sew side-pieced border strips in place. Trim off excess fabric (Figure 1). Repeat for top and bottom pieced border strips.

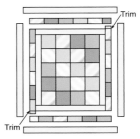

Figure 1

Sew on outer side borders, and then outer top and bottom borders.

Sandwich batting between backing fabric and pieced top. Quilt as desired using multicoloured cotton thread. Trim edges of layers even.

Sew binding strips together and fold in half lengthwise, wrong sides together. Sew to right side of quilt with raw edges even. Fold binding to wrong side of quilt and hand-stitch or stitch in the ditch folded edge to quilt. ■

BABY BLOCK PLAY MAT

This dresser play mat is a simple quilt accented with fusible appliqué.

Design | Connie Kauffman

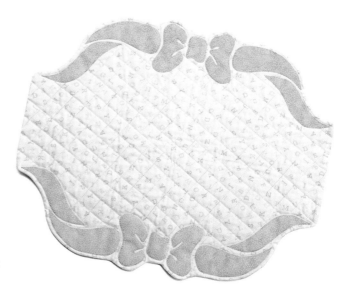

Project Specifications
Skill Level: Beginner
Mat Size: 21" x 18"

Materials
2 fat quarters cotton fabric each pastel baby print
1 fat quarter cotton fabric pink or blue print
Batting 22" x 19"
Fusible transfer web 12" x 12"
Coordinating variegated all-purpose thread

Instructions
Prepare templates using patterns given. Referring to Machine Appliqué (see page 12), make ribbon appliqués from pink or blue fat quarter. Remove paper backing.

Iron pastel, baby-print fat quarters. Place one fat quarter face up. Referring to photo for placement, position appliqués on fat quarter so they are at least ½" from edge of fabric. Fuse in place following manufacturer's instructions. Stitch around edges of each appliqué using blanket stitch and variegated thread.

Place quilt batting on flat surface. Place second baby print fat quarter and appliquéd mat top, right sides together, on quilt batting. Pin all layers together.

Sew around edges of mat, stitching ¼" from appliqués across top and bottom, and making a straight seam along the two sides with a 3½" opening on one side for turning (Figure 1).

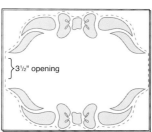

3½" opening

Figure 1

Trim seams. Turn mat right side out. Press under seam allowance at opening and hand stitch closed. Press mat.

To quilt, straight stitch around each appliqué and stitch between appliqués with crosshatch pattern, or as desired. ∎

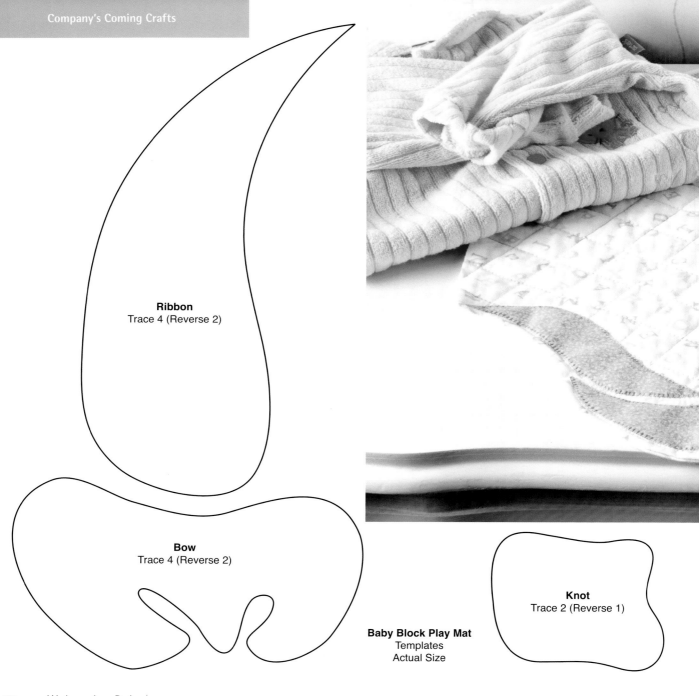

Ribbon
Trace 4 (Reverse 2)

Bow
Trace 4 (Reverse 2)

Knot
Trace 2 (Reverse 1)

Baby Block Play Mat
Templates
Actual Size

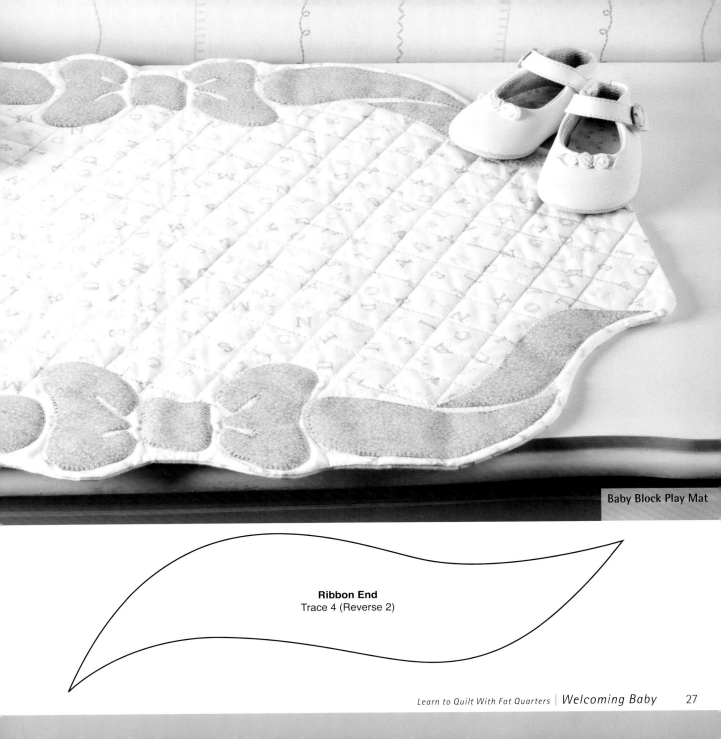

Ribbon End
Trace 4 (Reverse 2)

BABY BLOCKS WITH LOVE

The heart design in this quilt does not reveal itself until the blocks are sewn together in rows.

Design | Judith Sandstrom

Project Specifications

Skill Level: Beginner
Quilt Size: 40" x 56"
Block Size: 8" x 8"
Number of Blocks: 24

Materials

1 fat quarter each peach, green, orange and blue
 tone-on-tones
1 fat quarter blue print
½ yard blue print for binding
1 yard cream-on-cream print
1½ yards dark blue solid
Batting 44" x 60"
Backing 44" x 60"
All-purpose thread to match fabrics
Cream hand-quilting thread

Completing the Top

Cut two strips each 2½" x 40½" and 2½" x 48½" dark blue solid along the length of the fabric; set aside for borders.

Cut six 2½" x 22" strips from each tone-on-tone.

Cut eight 2½"-by-fabric-width strips cream-on-cream print. Cut each strip in half to make (16) 2½" x 21" strips. Subcut three of these strips into 2½" squares for A; you will need 24 A squares.

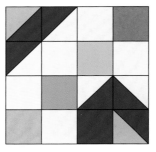

Block A
8" x 8" Block
Make 12

Block B
8" x 8" Block
Make 12

Cut three strips dark blue solid 2½" x 21"; subcut into 24 squares 2½" x 2½" for A.

Sew one tone-on-tone strip to one cream-on-cream print strip with right sides together along length; repeat for three of each colour tone-on-tone. Press seams toward darker fabric.

Subcut each strip set into 2½" segments to make B units as shown in Figure 1; you will need 24 B units of each tone-on-tone fabric.

Figure 1

Baby Blocks With Love

Stitch one strip of each tone-on-tone with right sides together along length to make a strip set; press seams in one direction. Repeat for three strip sets. Subcut each strip set into 2½" segments to make C units as shown in Figure 2; you will need 20 C units.

Figure 2

Cut seven strips cream-on-cream print, four strips blue print and 11 strips dark blue solid 2⅞" x 21". Subcut each strip into 2⅞" square segments; you will need 48 squares cream-on-cream print, 24 squares blue print and 72 squares dark blue solid. Cut each square in half on one diagonal to make D triangles.

Stitch each blue print D to a dark blue solid D to make a D unit as shown in Figure 3; repeat for all blue print D triangles. Repeat with remaining dark blue solid D triangles and cream-on-cream print D triangles, again referring to Figure 3.

Make 48   Make 96

Figure 3

Arrange the A squares and B and D units in rows, referring to Figure 4 for Blocks A and B. Join units in rows; join rows to complete one block. Repeat for 12 each A and B blocks; press seams open.

Block A   Block B

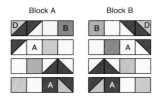

Figure 4

Arrange blocks in six rows of four blocks each, alternating the A and B blocks as shown in Figure 5. Join blocks in rows; press seams open. Join rows to complete the quilt centre; press seams open.

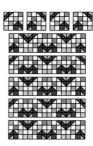

Figure 5

Join four C units to make a border strip; repeat for two strips. Join six C units to make a side border strip; repeat for two strips.

Sew a 2½" x 48½" strip dark blue solid to one six-unit side border strip; press seams away from the pieced strip. Repeat for two strips. Sew a strip to opposite sides of the pieced centre with the dark blue solid strip on the inside edge, referring to Figure 6; press seams toward dark blue solid strip. Repeat on the opposite long side of the quilt centre.

2½" x 48½"

Figure 6

Cut four squares 2½" x 2½" each blue print and dark blue solid. Sew a dark blue solid square and a blue print square to each end of the four-unit strips as shown in Figure 7. Sew a 2½" x 40½" strip dark blue solid to each pieced strip; press seams toward dark blue solid strips. Sew a strip to the top and bottom of the pieced centre; press seams toward dark blue solid strips.

Figure 7

Finishing the Quilt

Prepare quilt for quilting and quilt as desired, referring to Getting Ready to Quilt (see page 14). *Note: The sample shown was hand-quilted around the heart shapes and in a diagonal line through the centre of each block and in the ditch of border seams using cream hand-quilting thread.*

Prepare 5¾ yards self-made, blue-print binding and apply, referring to Finishing the Edges (see page 16). ■

Baby Blocks With Love
Placement Diagram
40" x 56"

2" x 40"

STITCHED WITH LOVE QUILT & TOTE

Use pretty batik fabrics for a simple block baby quilt and matching tote.

Designs | Carolyn Vagts

Project Specifications
Skill Level: Easy
Quilt Size: 46" x 58"
Tote Size: 12¼" x 9½" x 2"

Materials
6 each peach and lavender fat quarters in lightweight, woven fabric
¼ yard peach lightweight woven fabric
½ yard lavender lightweight woven fabric
3 yards lightweight woven fabric for quilt backing
¾ yard lightweight woven fabric for tote lining and pocket
Batting 52" x 64" and 25" x 35"

Quilt

Cutting
Note: Reserve fat-quarter scraps for tote.

From peach fat quarters, cut (16) 2½" x 20" strips. Cut (24) 6⅞" squares; cut each square in half diagonally. Cut four 4" squares for corners.

From lavender fat quarters, cut (16) 2½" x 20" strips. Cut (24) 6⅞" squares; cut each square in half diagonally.

From ¼ yard peach fabric, cut five 1½" strips the width of the fabric for first border.

From ½ yard lavender fabric, cut six 2½" strips the width of the fabric for binding.

Completing the Quilt
Sew one peach and one lavender half-square triangle together along the diagonal cut. Press seam open. Repeat to make a total of 48 blocks.

Lay out blocks into groups of four with all the peach sections on the inside (Figure 1). Sew the top two blocks together, then the bottom two, and then sew the top and bottom units together to make 12 block units. Press.

Figure 1

Referring to Figure 2, arrange block units in four rows of three units each. Sew three units together to make a row, and then sew rows together to complete centre of quilt.

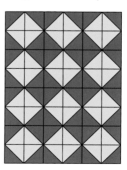

Figure 2

Stitched With Love Quilt & Tote

Sew peach borders to top and bottom of centre, and then sew to sides (Figure 3), piecing strips as needed and trimming to fit.

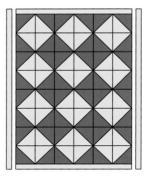

Figure 3

Sew four of the 2½" x 20" strips together along the 20" sides, alternating peach and lavender to make eight groups of 8½" x 20" units. Press. Crosscut units into (24) 4" sections (Figure 4). *Note: Remainder of units will be used for tote.*

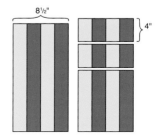

Figure 4

Sew five pieced units together to make the top border (Figure 5). Repeat to make the bottom border. Remove one end unit. Sew in place.

Figure 5

Sew seven pieced units together to make each side unit; remove three end units, and sew a 4" corner square to each end (Figure 6). Sew in place.

Figure 6

Layer batting between quilt top and backing fabric. Pin or baste together. Trim layers even. Quilt as desired.

Join binding strips diagonally and trim seam allowance (Figure 7). Press binding in half along length with wrong sides together. Unfold one end and trim it at a 45-degree angle, and then turn under the edge ½". Refold and press it back again (Figure 8).

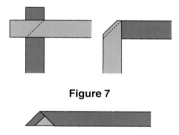

Figure 7

Figure 8

Referring to Finishing the Edges (see page 16), bind edges of quilt.

Tote

Cutting

From peach fat quarters, cut eight 3⅞" squares; cut each square in half diagonally to make 16 triangles. Cut four 12½" x 1½" strips, and four 8½" x 1½" strips.

From lavender fat quarters, cut eight 3⅞" squares; cut each square in half diagonally to make 16 triangles. Cut two 14½" x 2½" strips, and two 10½" x 2½" strips.

From remaining four-section units, cut four 8½" x 2½" sections for top band, and eight 8½" x 4½" sections for handles.

From fabric for tote lining and pocket, cut one 33" x 12½" rectangle for pocket.

From batting, cut one 33" x 12½" rectangle for tote, one 33" x 6½" rectangle for pocket, and two 2" x 32" strips for handles.

Completing the Tote

Sew one peach and one lavender half-square triangle together along the diagonal cut. Press seam open. Repeat to make a total of 16 blocks.

Referring to Figure 1 (see page 32) of Quilt, lay out blocks into groups of four with all the peach sections on the inside. Sew the top two blocks together, then the bottom two, and then sew the top and bottom units together to make 4 block units. Press.

Sew two units together (Figure 9). Repeat with remaining two units. These are the centres for the front and back of the tote.

Figure 9

Sew a 12½" x 1½" strip to the top and bottom of each unit. Sew an 8½" x 1½" strip to each side of each unit (Figure 10).

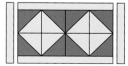

Figure 10

Sew a 14½" x 2½" strip across the bottom of the front and the back, and sew a 10½" x 2½" strip to the right side of each unit (Figure 11).

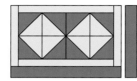

Figure 11

Sew both units together to make one long unit (Figure 12).

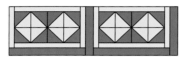

Figure 12

Sew the 2½" four-section units together to make a strip and sew across the top of the unit (Figure 13). Trim four-section unit to fit pieced tote unit. Use pieced unit as a pattern to cut lining fabric. Set lining aside.

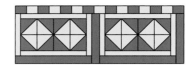

Figure 13

Pin or baste batting to the wrong side of the joined unit and stitch in the ditch around blocks and borders to quilt.

Fold pocket rectangle in half with right sides together. Layer the 33" x 6½" piece of batting on one side and stitch through all thicknesses along long raw edges. Turn pocket rectangle right side out with batting sandwiched between. Press. Topstitch along seamed (top) edge (Figure 14).

Figure 14

Position pocket on right side of lining with bottom of pocket 2½" from bottom of lining. Topstitch across bottom edge of pocket. Make vertical stitches to divide pocket (Figure 15).

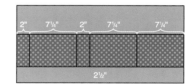

Figure 15

Sew four handle strips together to make one 32½"-long unit. Repeat with remaining four handle strips. Press each unit in half with right sides together, matching long edges. Layer a strip of batting on one side and sew along the long raw edges of each unit through all thicknesses. Turn handles right side out. Press.

Referring to Handle Placement Diagram, baste ends of handles to top edge of tote. Sew lining and tote with right sides together across top edge, catching ends of handles in stitching.

With right sides together and handles inside, fold tote and lining in half, matching sides. Stitch across bottom and side of tote, and across side and bottom of lining, leaving an opening in bottom of lining for turning.

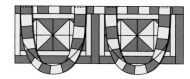

Stitched With Love Quilt & Tote
Handle Placement Diagram

Fold the bottom of the tote, matching the bottom seam with the side seams, and stitch across the bottom 1" from the points (Figure 16). Trim seam allowance. Repeat for the lining.

Figure 16

Turn the tote and lining right side out. Hand stitch the lining opening closed and fit lining into tote. Topstitch around top edge of tote. ■

BABY BIBS TWINS

Whether the new baby in your life is a boy or a girl, he or she will look perfect in this bib duo.

Designs | Lorine Mason

Project Specifications
Skill Level: Beginner
Bib Size: 8" x 7½"

Materials
5 fat quarters in coordinating pastels
Batting 10" x 10" for each bib
All-purpose thread to match fabrics
1 package extra-wide double-fold bias tape to coordinate with fabrics
1 yard picot trim
1 (½") aqua button
4 (⅝") pink buttons

Cutting
Prepare pattern for the bib; cut one piece of batting for each bib, cutting batting at least 1" larger than the shape all around. Mark a centreline from side to side on batting shape for a boy bib or from top to bottom for a girl bib.

Using the pattern, cut one backing piece for each bib from any fat quarter.

Prepare tie template; cut as directed.

Cut a 1¾" x 21" strip from each fat quarter.

Cut a 1" x 7" strip from one fat quarter for button placket.

Completing the It's a Boy Bib
Place one 1¾"-wide strip on the boy-bib batting shape along the marked centreline; place a second strip on top. Stitch and press strip to the right side as shown in Figure 1; trim strips even with batting.

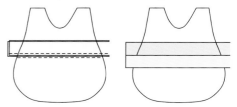

Figure 1

Repeat until batting piece is covered.

Lay the bib pattern on the patchwork top; trace around outside edges. Stitch along the edges of the traced lines.

Cut out the bib close to the outside edge of the stitched lines.

Pin the tie pieces right sides together; stitch around, leaving the top narrow edge open. Trim point and turn right side out; press flat.

Centre and pin the tie piece with narrow end even with neck edge; baste to hold.

Baby Bibs Twins

Stitch tie in place ⅛" from edge through all layers.

Place a bib backing piece with the wrong side against the batting side of the stitched unit and pin to hold layers together.

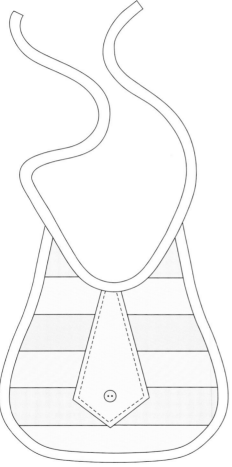

It's a Boy
Placement Diagram
8" x 7½"

Referring to Figure 2, enclose outside edges of bib with bias binding and topstitch through all layers using a decorative stitch such as a blanket stitch.

Figure 2

Cut a 30" length of bias binding for neck edge; centre the strip on the neck edge and stitch in place.

Sew a button to the centre of the tie to finish.

Completing the It's a Girl Bib

Cut an odd-shaped piece no larger than 3" from any one of the fat quarters. *Note: A five-sided shape is ideal; a pattern has been provided should you want to use it.*

Lay the piece right side up on the girl batting shape, placing slightly off-centre; pin to hold.

Cut a second piece of fabric at least as long as one of the sides of the first patch, plus ½"; lay this patch right sides together on top of the first patch, aligning the raw edges; pin and then stitch along raw edges as shown in Figure 3. Press the second piece to the right side and pin flat, referring to Figure 4.

Figure 3

Figure 4

Continue adding pieces in this manner, working in a clockwise direction, until the batting is covered.

Using a variety of decorative stitches, stitch along the seams between pieces.

Lay the bib pattern on the patchwork top; trace around outside edges. Stitch along the edges of the traced lines.

Cut out the bib close to the outside edge of the stitched lines.

Turn under ¼" along each long side of the 1" x 7" button placket strip; press.

Centre and pin the strip down the front of the bib. Insert and pin a 7" length of picot trim under each long side of the centre strip as shown in Figure 5.

Figure 5

Topstitch down each side of the strip through all layers as shown in Figure 6; trim strip even with bib edges.

Figure 6

Pin and baste an 8" length of picot trim along the curved neck area; trim to fit.

Bind edges as in Completing the It's a Boy Bib.

Evenly space and sew four buttons to the centre front of the bib to finish. ■

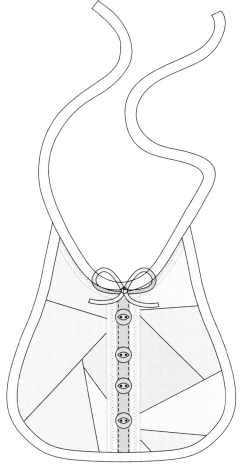

It's a Girl
Placement Diagram
8" x 7½"

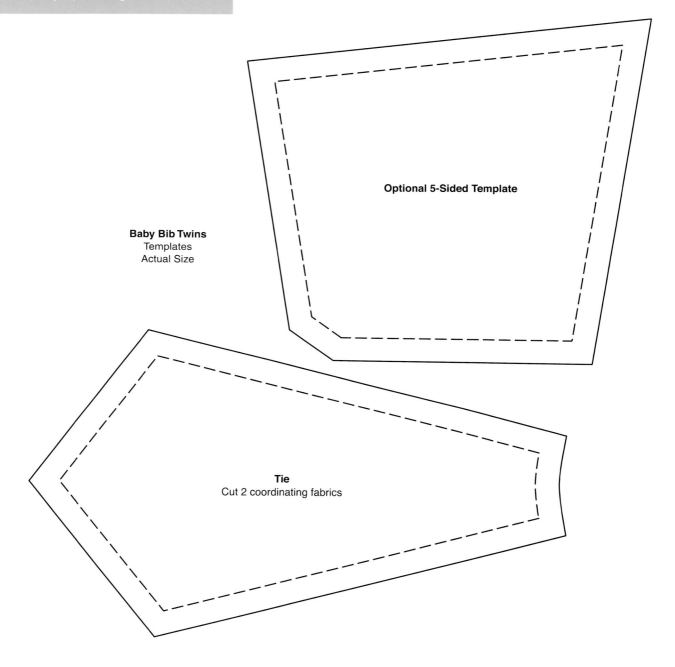

Optional 5-Sided Template

Baby Bib Twins
Templates
Actual Size

Tie
Cut 2 coordinating fabrics

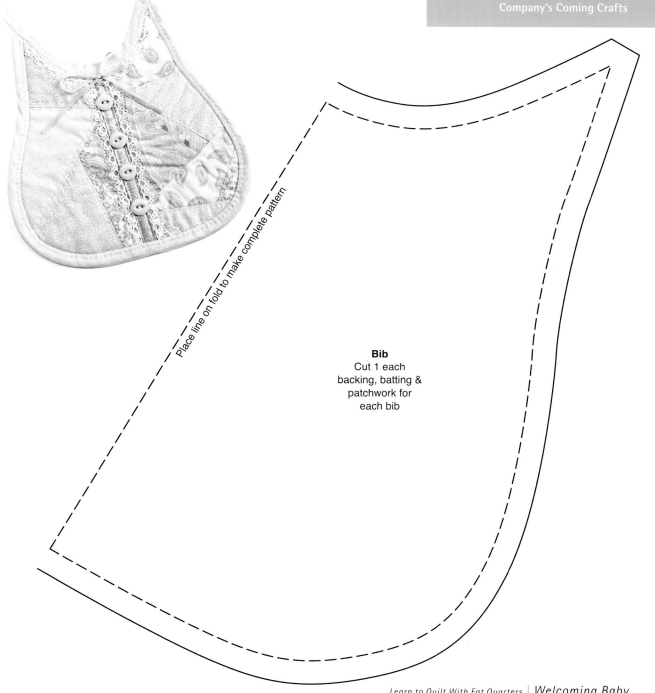

Place line on fold to make complete pattern

Bib
Cut 1 each
backing, batting &
patchwork for
each bib

DOWN ON THE FARM GIFT SET

Funky farm animals dance across this fun diaper backpack filled with a quilted changing pad and baby-wipes cover.

Designs | Lorine Mason

Project Specifications

Skill Level: Easy
Changing Pad Size: 22½" x 22½"
Backpack Size: 15" x 14½" x 2¼"
Baby-Wipes Cover Size: Varies

Materials

2 fat quarters cotton fabric each multicoloured large
   prints, blue medium prints and blue small prints
3 fat quarters each green prints and yellow prints
Fusible fleece 23½" square
2 yards ⅜"-wide woven braid or trim
Decorative button for pocket
Flat buttons: (6) ⅝" and 1 each ½" and ⅜"
Travel-size package of baby wipes

Changing Pad

Cutting

From multicoloured, large-print fat quarters, cut one
18" M square.

From blue, medium-print fat quarters, cut one 8¾" A square,
four 4" x 4¼" I rectangles and two 8" x 4¼" L rectangles.

From green-print fat quarters, cut three 1" D strips, one
1½" H strip and one 2" F strip, each the width of the fabric.

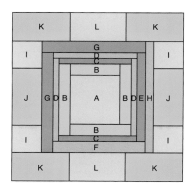

Changing Pad Front
Placement Diagram
22½" x 22½"

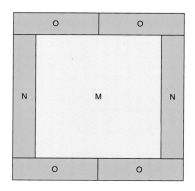

Changing Pad Back
Placement Diagram
22½" x 22½"

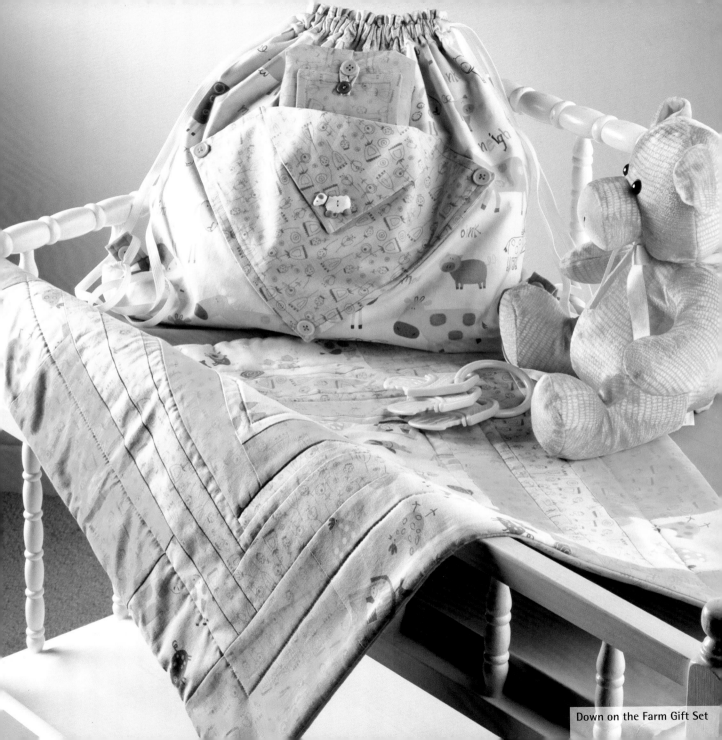

Down on the Farm Gift Set

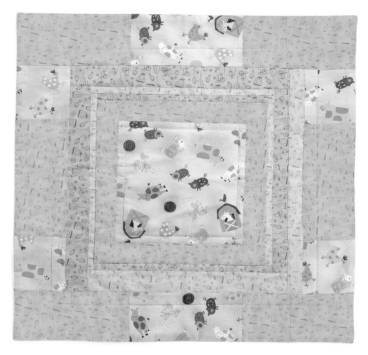

place. *Reserve a 4" length of 1"-wide blue, small-print strip for use in baby-wipes cover.* Sew two I pieces to each J piece and sew to each side of pieced front. Sew two K pieces to each L piece and sew across top and bottom to complete the front.

For back of changing pad, sew N strips to opposite sides of the M square. Sew short edges of two O pieces together. Repeat with remaining two O pieces. Sew joined strips across top and bottom of back unit as shown in Changing Pad Back Placement Diagram (see page 44).

Using a rotary cutter, trim ¼" from all sides of pad front, forming a square. Fuse the square of fleece to the wrong side of the pad back. With right sides together, centre pad front on top of the back and pin together.

Stitch together using a ½" seam allowance, leaving a 3" opening on one side. Turn right side out. Press. Hand stitch opening closed. Quilt as desired.

Backpack

Cutting
From multicoloured, large-print fat quarters, cut one 18" square for backpack front.

From blue, medium-print fat quarters, cut one 2" x 6" strip for tabs.

From green-print fat quarters, cut two 18" squares for lining front and back.

From blue, small-print fat quarters, cut two 10" squares for front pocket.

From yellow-print fat quarters, cut one 18" square for backpack back.

From blue, small-print fat quarters, cut two 1" C strips, one 1½" E strip and two 2" G strips, each the width of the fabric.

From yellow-print fat quarters, cut three 2" B strips the width of the fabric, four 8¼" x 4¼" K rectangles, two 8½" x 4¼" J rectangles, two 18" x 3¼" N strips and four 11¾" x 3¼" O strips.

Completing the Changing Pad
Referring to Changing Pad Front Placement Diagram (see page 44), assemble pieces A through H as shown, beginning with square A and working in a clockwise direction. *Note: Trim each strip to length as it is sewn into*

Completing the Backpack

Fold tab strip in half lengthwise, right sides together, and stitch along the 6" length. Turn right side out and topstitch along each edge. Cut in half and fold to form two tabs. Pin ends together.

Pin each tab to backpack front 2" from bottom, along sides, with raw edges even. Sew front and back together, along side and bottom edges, catching ends of tabs in stitching. Flatten bottom of bag, matching bottom seam to side seams on each side. Sew across bottom 1" from point on each side to box bottom. Trim seam allowance. Turn bag right side out.

Stitch lining front and back, along side and bottom edges. Box bottom of lining in same manner as for bag. Slip lining inside bag, wrong sides together, matching seams and top edges. Pin. Fold top edge 1¾" to the front of the bag and press well. Pin. Topstitch through all layers of

fabric ¼" from the folded edge and again 1" from the first stitching to form a casing for the drawstrings.

Sew front-pocket squares with right sides together, leaving a 2" opening on one side. Turn right side out and press. Fold over one corner to form a flap and press well. Centre pocket on the front of the bag and pin in place. Stitch along sides and bottom edges of pocket through all layers of fabric.

Remove stitching in casing side seams from the first two layers of fabric only. Cut braid into 1-yard lengths. Thread one length of braid through from one side, bringing both ends out on opposite side. Thread the second length through from the opposite side to make draw strings. Tie each end through the tab on each side and knot.

Sew a decorative button to the pocket flap. Sew a ⅝" button to each corner of the pocket and to each tab.

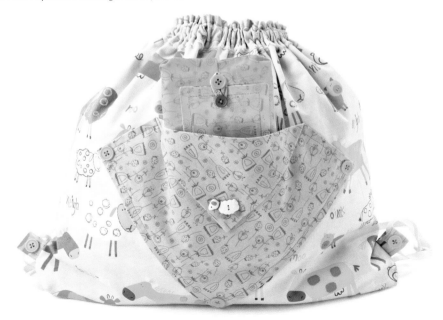

Baby-Wipes Cover

Instructions

Measure the length and width of the package of baby wipes. Add 1" to the length and 2" to the width. Cut a piece of yellow-print fabric this length and width for cover bottom.

Cut a second piece of yellow print the same length as the cover bottom, but 2" wider. Fold in half, matching long edges, and cut down the centre for cover top pieces. Turn over and press in 1" on one long edge of each piece. Double topstitch close to the raw edge. Pin top cover pieces to bottom cover, right sides together, across the top and bottom edges. Set aside.

Using the same length measurement as cover bottom and a 4" width, cut one piece of yellow print and one piece of medium, blue-print fabric for the flap. Sew pieces with right sides together using a ¼" seam allowance, leaving the top edge open. Turn right side out and press. Topstitch ¼" away from stitched edges.

Remove the pins from the cover top/bottom and insert flap with underside of flap against the right side of the cover top. Pin. Stitch around edges of cover using a ½" seam allowance. Clip corners. Turn right side out. Press.

Fold reserved 4"-long blue, small-print strip in half lengthwise (from Changing Pad), matching long edges. Sew long edges together using a ¼" seam allowance. Turn right side out. Press. Fold strip in half to form a loop. Attach ends of loop to centre bottom of flap by sewing ⅜" button through them. Sew ⅝" button to cover top to correspond with loop. *Note: Sew button to both halves of opening.*

Insert baby wipes in cover. Draw loop over button to close flap. ■

SUMMER DELIGHT RUNNER

A simple-to-sew quilted table runner accented with yo-yos is perfect for your summer table.

Design | Patsy Moreland

Project Specifications
Skill Level: Beginner
Runner Size: 12" x 32"

Materials
1 fat quarter each floral/fruit print, blue print,
   brown print, light green print and green print
2 fat quarters mottled prints for borders and strips
1 yard multicoloured fusible bias tape to coordinate
   with fabrics
Batting 12" x 32"
Small yo-yo maker (1¼" finished size)

Cutting
From floral/fruit print fat quarter, cut two 4½" squares
on wrong side of fabric. On right side of fabric, cut
two 8½" x 4½" rectangles and two 2½" x 22" strips
for backing.

Following yo-yo manufacturer's instructions, cut squares
to make six small yo-yos from floral/fruit print.

From blue print fat quarter, cut three 4½" squares;
cut two 2½" x 22" strips for backing.

From brown print fat quarter, cut two 4½" squares and
two 2½" x 22" strips for backing.

From light green print fat quarter, cut one 4½" square and
two 2½" x 22" strips for backing.

From green print fat quarter, cut two 6½" x 4½"
rectangles and two 2½" x 22" strips for backing.

From mottled print fat quarters for borders and strips, cut
two 2½" x 10½" F strips. Cut one 2½" x 30½" G strip and
two 2½" x 34½" H strips, piecing each strip as needed.

Completing the Runner
Referring to Assembly Diagrams (see page 50) for
placement, piece together strips 1 and 2. Sew strips 1 and
2 to edges of G strip. Sew F strips to ends of pieced unit.
Sew H strips across top and bottom edges.

For backing, sew 2½"-wide strips together in random patterns. Cut across seams at 2½" intervals (Figure 1). Sew strips back together to form pieced backing of 15 rows of five blocks each.

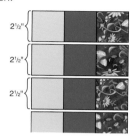

Figure 1

Place pieced front wrong side up. Centre craft batting on wrong side of the front. Centre the pieced backing on the batting with right side up. Pin through all layers.

Turn under raw edge of extended border ¼". Fold border edge over pieced backing and pin in place, mitring corners. Press. Hand- or machine-stitch to backing.

Referring to photo for placement, fuse bias tape across centre front strip. Make yo-yos following manufacturer's instructions. Hand-stitch yo-yos 3"–5" apart on top of bias tape. ■

Strip 1

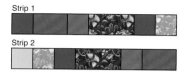

Strip 2

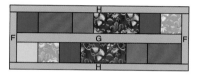

Summer Delight Runner
Assembly Diagrams

Summer Delight Runner

PINK & GREEN SQUARED

Sew a pieced table runner to give as a special hostess gift, and you'll always be invited back.

Design | Rochelle Martin

Project Specifications
Skill Level: Beginner
Quilt Size: 36" x 12"

Materials
1 fat quarter each black dots, green dots and pink dots
⅜ yard black-and-white print for squares and binding
¾ yard light green print for squares and backing
⅓ yard 17"-wide lightweight paper-backed fusible web
Craft-size thin cotton batting
Optional: free-motion foot

Cutting
Cut 28 squares each 2½" from black-dot fat quarter.

Cut three 2¼" x 22" strips from green-dot fat quarter.

Cut two 1¾" x 22" strips from pink-dot fat quarter.

From black-and-white print, cut 28 squares each 2½".
Cut three 2" strips the width of the fabric for binding.

From light green print, cut 13 squares each 4½". Cut
one 14" x 40" rectangle for backing.

From fusible web, cut three 2" strips and two 1½" strips
each the width of the fusible web.

Pink & Green
4" x 4" Block
Make 14

Making Four-Patch Blocks
Sew a black-and-white print 2½" square to a black-dot
2½" square (Figure 1). Press seam open. Repeat to make
28 units.

Figure 1

Pink & Green Squared

Sew two units together to make 14 Four-Patch blocks, matching centre seams (Figure 2). Press seams open.

Figure 2

Adding Fancy Squares

Fuse the three 2" strips of paper-backed fusible web centred on the wrong sides of the 2¼" x 22" green-dot strips (Figure 3).

Figure 3

Use rotary cutter and ruler to trim each strip to 1½" x 17" (Figure 4). Cut (28) 1½" green-dot squares from the strips (Figure 5).

Figure 4

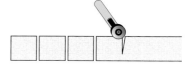

Figure 5

Fuse 1½" strips of fusible web to pink-dot strips in same manner; trim fused strips to 1" wide. Cut (28) 1" pink-dot squares.

Remove paper backing from two green-dot and two pink-dot squares. Fuse to Four-Patch block as shown in block diagram (see page 52). Repeat to make 14 appliquéd blocks.

Completing the Runner

Referring to Placement Diagram, lay out appliquéd blocks and 4½" light green print squares in a 3" x 9"-block format, turning some blocks as shown.

Sew blocks into three long rows. Press seams open between blocks. Sew the three rows together, matching seams. Press open long row seams.

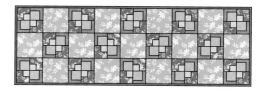

Pink & Green Squared
Placement Diagram
36" x 12"

Layer table runner top, batting and backing, and baste for machine quilting. Stipple or quilt as desired in light green print blocks.

Quilt appliquéd blocks using a decorative stitch on edges of fused squares, beginning by stitching around green squares (Figure 6), and then stitching around remaining edges of pink squares separately.

Sew edges of binding strips together; press. Fold binding lengthwise, wrong sides together and press. With right sides together and raw edges even, stitch binding to front of runner, mitring corners. Fold binding over raw edges and hand-stitch to backing. ■

Start Here

Figure 6

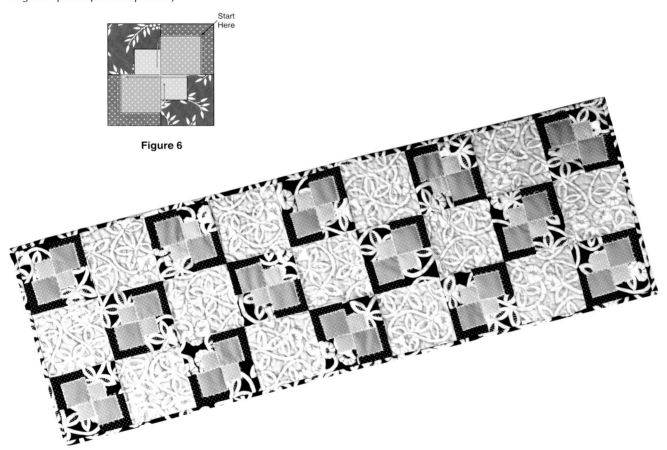

SUNFLOWER SENSATION

Add interest to a pieced table runner with embroidered panels or a purchased appliqué that echo the design of the main fabric.

Design | Carol Zentgraf

Project Specifications

Skill Level: Easy
Runner Size: 66" x 15", excluding tassels

Materials

6 brown sunflower print Batik fat quarters
2 orange print Batik fat quarters
1 yellow print Batik fat quarter
8 yards ⅝"-wide brown gimp trim
2 (4") brown tassels
3 (9" x 12") sheets double-sided fusible transfer web
Embroidery machine with sunflower embroidery design*
Optional: rayon machine-embroidery thread
Tear-away stabilizer
Optional: permanent fabric adhesive

*A purchased appliqué in coordinating colours may be substituted for machine embroidery.

Cutting

From brown sunflower print fat quarters, cut two 22" x 16" rectangles for centre top, and four 17½" x 16" rectangles for backing.

From orange print fat quarters, cut one 10" square for centre top, and two 13" x 16" rectangles for top end panels.

From yellow print fat quarter, cut two 9" squares for embroidered panels.

Completing the Runner

With stabilizer on wrong side of each yellow print 9" square, embroider or machine-appliqué a sunflower in centre. Tear away excess stabilizer.

Sunflower Sensation

Sew short edges of 22" x 16" centre top rectangles together. Sew an orange end panel to each end of the centre. Press seams open.

Apply fusible web to wrong sides of orange centre square and two embroidered/appliquéd yellow squares. Remove paper backings. Position orange square on point in centre of runner top (Figure 1). Position each embroidered square on point in centre of each end panel (Figure 2). Fuse in place.

Figure 1

Figure 2

Trim end rectangles even with outer edges of embroidered squares, continuing line to side edges to make end points (Figure 3).

Figure 3

Sew or glue gimp trim over all edges of centre square, the two inner edges of embroidered squares, and the end panel seams.

Sew short edges of back rectangles together, leaving an 8" opening in centre of one seam for turning. Press seams open. Pin top and back together. Trim ends of back to fit top. Sew together along outer edges. Turn right side out through back seam opening. Press. Slipstitch opening closed.

Cut hanging loop of each tassel to 1½". Apply adhesive to cut ends to prevent ravelling. Sew or glue gimp trim around outer edges of runner top, inserting tassel loop ends under gimp at each end point. ■

CHERRY PICKIN'

Celebrate spring by stitching this cheerful runner and placemats set. Every meal will become a special occasion.

Designs | Barbara Miller from Brenda/Barb Designs

Project Specifications
Skill Level: Beginner
Runner Size: 58" x 18"
Placemat Size: 18" x 12"

Materials
Scraps red mottleds and green mottleds and tonals
6 coordinating fat quarters
1 fat quarter each light, medium and dark green mottleds
⅜ yard white tonal
⅞ yard darkest green mottled
Batting 66" x 26" and (2) 22" x 16"
Backing 66" x 26" and (2) 22" x 16"
All-purpose thread to match fabrics and brown
Quilting thread
¼ yard lightweight fusible web

Cutting for Runner
Cut three 2½"-by-fabric-width strips white tonal; subcut strips into two strips each of the following: 24½" A, 10½" B, 6½" C and 4½" D.

Cut 22 total 4½" x 4½" F squares from the coordinating fat quarters.

Cut two 4½" x 20½" G strips each light, medium and dark green mottleds.

Cut one 6½"-by-fabric-width strip darkest green mottled; subcut into one 6½" E square. Cut two 2¼" strips from the remaining width for binding.

Cut three 2¼"-by-fabric-width strips darkest green mottled for additional binding.

Cutting for 2 Placemats
Cut one 2½"-by-fabric-width strip white tonal; subcut strip into two 12½" H strips.

Cut two 4½" x 12½" I strips each light, medium and dark green mottleds.

Cut six 4½" x 4½" F squares from coordinating fat quarters.

Cut four 2¼"-by-fabric-width strips darkest green mottled for binding.

Completing the Runner

Sew an F square to one end of each G strip; press seams on half toward F and half toward G.

Join one each light, medium and dark green F-G strips, alternating seam pressing to make an F-G unit as shown in Figure 1. Repeat to make two F-G units.

Figure 1

Join six F squares to make an F strip; press seams in one direction. Repeat to make two F strips.

Join one F-G unit and an F strip with an A strip to complete one end unit of the runner as shown in Figure 2; press seams away from the A strip. Repeat to make a second end unit.

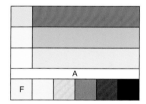

Figure 2

Sew C to opposite sides of E; press seams toward E. Sew B to the top and bottom of E to complete the E unit as shown in Figure 3; press seams toward E.

Figure 3

Join two F squares with D at one end to make a D-F unit as shown in Figure 4; press seams away from D. Repeat to make two D-F units.

Figure 4

Sew a D-F unit to opposite sides of the E unit to complete the centre unit as shown in Figure 5; press seams away from the E unit.

Figure 5

Sew an end unit to each long side of the centre unit to complete the piecing of the runner top.

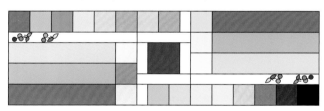

Cherry Pickin' Runner
Placement Diagram
58" x 18"

Appliquéing Cherry Motifs

Trace appliqué shapes onto the paper side of the fusible web, leaving ½" between shapes, as directed on pattern; cut out shapes, leaving a margin around each one.

Fuse shapes to the wrong side of fabrics as directed on pieces for colour; cut out shapes on traced lines. Remove paper backing.

Cherry Pickin'

Arrange and fuse appliqué motifs on each A strip, referring to the Placement Diagram (see page 60) and the appliqué motif pattern for positioning.

Using brown thread, machine-stitch several lines of decorative stitching to create the stems between cherries and leaves.

Using thread to match fabrics, machine blanket-stitch around each leaf and cherry shape to complete the runner top.

Completing the Placemats

To make one placemat, join three I strips along length to make an I unit; press seams in one direction.

Join three F squares to make an F unit; press seams in one direction.

Join the I and F units with H, referring to the Placement Diagram; press seams away from H to complete the placemat piecing.

Prepare and add appliqué motifs to H, referring to Appliquéing Cherry Motifs.

Repeat to complete two placemat tops.

Cherry Pickin' Placemat
Placement Diagram
18" x 12"

Completing the Runner & Placemats

Sandwich the batting pieces between the completed tops and prepared backing pieces; pin or baste layers together.

Quilt as desired by hand or machine. When quilting is complete, trim batting and backing even with edges of the quilted tops.

Join binding strips on short ends with diagonal seams to make one long strip; trim seams to ¼" and press seams open. *Note: You may join the runner strips to make one strip and the placemat strips to make a separate strip, or join them all to make one continuous strip to be used for all projects.*

Fold binding strip in half wrong sides together along length; press.

Sew binding to the right side of each top, matching raw edges, mitring corners and overlapping ends; press binding away from quilt edges and turn to the back side. Hand- or machine-stitch in place to finish. ■

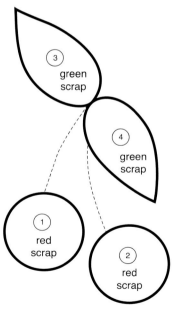

2-Cherry Motif
Prepare 2 for runner &
1 for each place mat

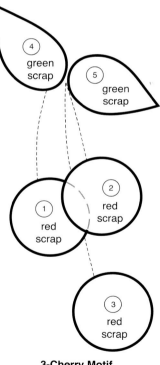

3-Cherry Motif
Prepare 2 for runner &
1 for each place mat

POSY COZY & COASTERS

You'll love to sew this appliquéd floral tea cozy and matching coasters for your next afternoon tea party.

Designs | Chris Malone

Project Specifications
Skill Level: Beginner
Cozy Size: 14½" x 11½"
Coaster Size: 4½" x 4½"

Materials
4 fat quarters coordinating light tan prints
1 fat quarter each dark tan print (for basket appliqué, coaster backings and borders), green print and red print
Batting: 2 rectangles each 11½" x 14½" and 4 squares each 5" x 5"
1 yard ⅛" piping cord
1 yard light tan single-fold bias tape
Tan buttons: 4 (¾") and 4 (½")
Paper-backed fusible transfer web

Cutting
From each of four coordinating light tan print fat quarters, cut two 6" x 7½" rectangles for tea cozy front and back; cut one 4" x 4" square for coaster fronts.

From one of the four coordinating light tan print fat quarters, cut two 11½" x 14½" rectangles for tea cozy lining.

From dark tan print fat quarter, cut four 5" x 5" squares for coaster backing, and eight 1" x 4" strips and eight 1" x 5" strips for coaster borders.

From green print fat quarter, cut two 1⅛" x 20" bias strips for piping.

Enlarge Posy Cozy & Coasters templates as indicated and prepare templates using enlarged patterns. Referring to Machine Appliqué (see page 12), make one basket appliqué from dark tan print, four cozy leaf appliqués from green print, eight coaster leaf appliqués (reversing four) from green print, three cozy flowers from red print, and four coaster flowers from red print.

Completing the Cozy
Sew tea cozy front/back rectangles together in pairs along short edges. Press seams. Sew two pairs together to make a tea cozy front and a back, matching seams. Press.

Remove paper backing from tea cozy appliqué pieces and fuse in place on tea cozy front, using photo as a guide for placement. Blanket-stitch edges of all appliqués by hand or machine.

Posy Cozy & Coasters

Fold tea cozy back in half. Using a dinner plate or similar object as a template, round the top corners (Figure 1). Using tea cozy back as a pattern, cut tea cozy front, both tea cozy lining pieces and both 11½" x 14½" batting rectangles to match.

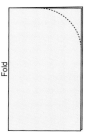

Fold

Figure 1

Place one cozy lining wrong side up with one batting piece on top. Smooth the cozy front in place with right side up; pin. Machine-baste all around just inside seam allowance. Repeat with cozy back.

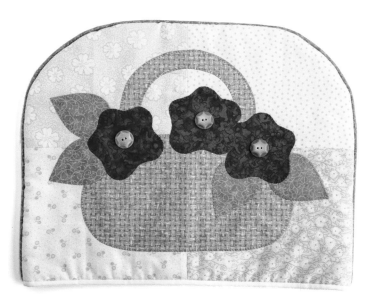

On cozy front, sew a ¾" button to centre of each flower, sewing through all layers. On cozy back, sew a ¾" button to centre of patchwork back through all layers.

Join bias strips with a diagonal seam (Figure 2). Trim seam to ¼" and press open. Wrap piping cord with bias strips and sew close to cord using a zipper foot. With raw edges even, pin piping to curved edge of cozy front. Machine-baste close to cord.

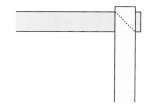

Figure 2

Pin cozy front and back together with right sides facing and raw edges even. Stitching from the wrong side of the cozy front so you can see the basting, stitch the layers together just inside the previous stitching line. Serge or zigzag seam edges to finish. Turn right side out.

Unfold bias tape and turn under short end ¼". Beginning at back raw edge of cozy, sew tape to lower edge, stitching in the fold line with the raw edges even (Figure 3). Overlap end and trim excess. Wrap bias tape over raw edge to inside of cozy and slipstitch in place.

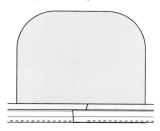

Figure 3

Completing the Coasters

Referring to photo for placement, fuse one coaster flower and two coaster leaves to each coaster front, taking care to keep each motif ⅝" from the outside edge. Blanket-stitch around appliqué pieces by hand or machine.

Sew a 4" border strip to each side of an appliquéd front; press seams outward. Sew a 5" border strip to the top and bottom; press seams outward.

Pin coaster front and back, right sides together, to a 5" batting square. Sew around edges, leaving a 2½" opening on one side. Trim corners. Trim batting close to seam to reduce bulk. Turn right side out.

Fold in seam allowance on opening and slipstitch closed. Stitch in the ditch on front of coaster to quilt. Sew a ½" button to centre of each flower through all layers. ∎

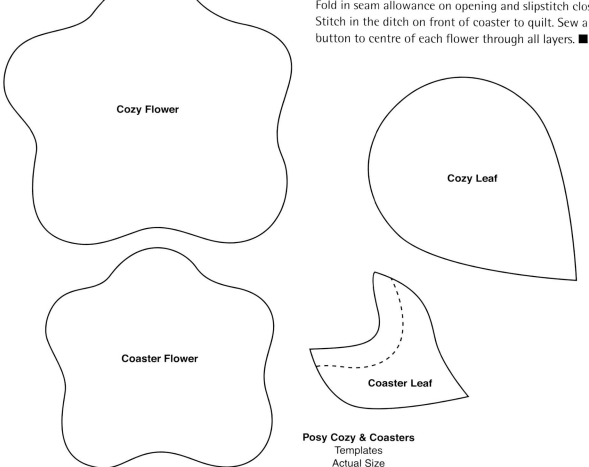

Cozy Flower

Cozy Leaf

Coaster Flower

Coaster Leaf

Posy Cozy & Coasters
Templates
Actual Size

Basket
Template
Enlarge 125%

FLORAL SILHOUETTES

Pieced spool blocks are the vases for the stitched and appliquéd flowers in this simple quilted runner.

Design | Leslie Beck

Project Specifications
Skill Level: Beginner
Quilt Size: 24" x 15½"
Block Size: 4" x 4"
Number of Blocks: 4

Materials
Scraps of green and rose prints, solids or mottleds
1 fat quarter each rose, navy, green and purple
    tone-on-tones
1 fat quarter cream-on-cream print
¼ yard blue tone-on-tone for border
¼ yard dark rose print for binding
Batting 28" x 20"
Backing 28" x 20"
All-purpose thread to match fabrics
Cream machine-quilting thread
Green, purple, blue and pink 6-strand embroidery floss
¼ yard lightweight fusible transfer web
4 (½") coloured buttons
Water-erasable marker or pencil

Instructions
Trace flower motif pieces onto the paper side of the lightweight fusible transfer web as directed on the pattern for number to cut.

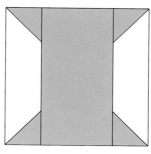

Spool
4" x 4" Block
Make 4

Cut out shapes, leaving a margin around each one. Fuse each shape to the wrong side of fabrics as directed on each piece for colour; cut out shapes on traced line. Remove paper backing.

Cut a 7" x 19½" rectangle cream-on-cream print for background.

Measure in 6¾" from the left side edge and mark as shown in Figure 1.

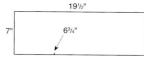

Figure 1

Position the flower motif stem at the mark; slip leaf shapes under stem, referring to the pattern for placement; fuse in place. Arrange and fuse remaining pieces in numerical order, referring to the pattern; set aside.

To piece the Spool blocks, cut one 2½" x 4½" rectangle from each tone-on-tone fat quarter for A.

Cut (11) 1½" x 4½" rectangles cream-on-cream print for B; set aside three B pieces for sashing strips.

Cut four 1½" x 1½" squares from each tone-on-tone fat quarter for C. Mark a diagonal line from corner to corner on the wrong side of each C square.

Place a C square right sides together with B as shown in Figure 2; stitch on marked line. Trim excess seam to ¼"; press C to the right side.

Figure 2

Repeat with a matching fabric C on the opposite end of B to complete a B-C unit as shown in Figure 3; repeat for eight B-C units.

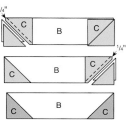

Figure 3

Sew a B-C unit to opposite long sides of A, matching C colour with A as shown in Figure 4 to complete one Spool block; repeat for four blocks.

Figure 4

Trace four star shapes onto the paper side of the lightweight fusible transfer web; cut out shapes, leaving a margin around each one. Fuse to fabrics as directed on piece. Cut out fused star shapes on traced lines; remove paper backing.

Fuse a star shape to the centre of each A piece on each Spool block, referring to the Placement Diagram (see page 72) for colour placement.

Machine buttonhole-stitch around each star shape using all-purpose thread to match fabrics; repeat with fused flower shapes.

Join the blocks with the remaining B pieces as shown in Figure 5 to complete the pieced section.

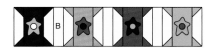

Figure 5

Sew the appliquéd section to the pieced section to complete the centre; press seam away from pieced section.

Mark the stitching motif pattern given in the empty background above the three Spool blocks, referring to the Placement Diagram (see page 72) for positioning.

Floral Silhouettes

Using two strands green embroidery floss, backstitch along marked lines for leaves and stems. Repeat with blue, pink and purple embroidery floss for flowers, referring to the Placement Diagram (see page 72) for colour placement.

Make French knots in the flower centres, as shown in Figure 6, using embroidery floss to match flower tops.

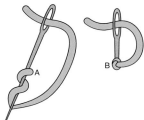

Figure 6

Cut two strips each 1" x 11" and 1" x 20½" rose tone-on-tone. Sew the shorter strips to opposite short sides and the longer strips to opposite long sides; press seams toward strips.

Cut two strips each 2½" x 12" and 2½" x 24½" blue tone-on-tone. Sew the shorter strips to opposite short sides and the longer strips to opposite long sides; press seams toward strips.

Prepare for quilting and quilt as desired, referring to Getting Ready to Quilt (see page 14). *Note: The sample shown was machine-quilted in the cream-on-cream background areas with a meandering design using cream machine-quilting thread. The borders were stitched in the ditch using all-purpose thread to match fabrics.*

Prepare 2¾ yards self-made dark rose print binding and apply, referring to Finishing the Edges (see page 16).

Sew a button in the centre of each star to finish. ■

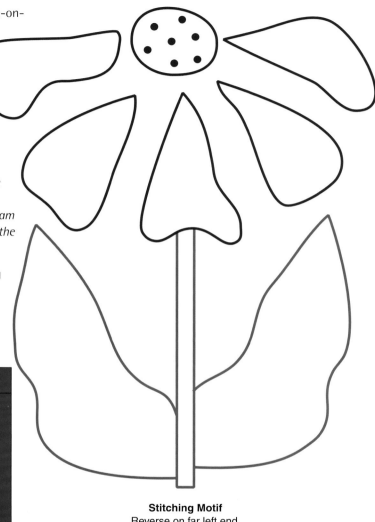

Stitching Motif
Reverse on far left end.

Floral Silhouettes
Placement Diagram
24" x 15½"

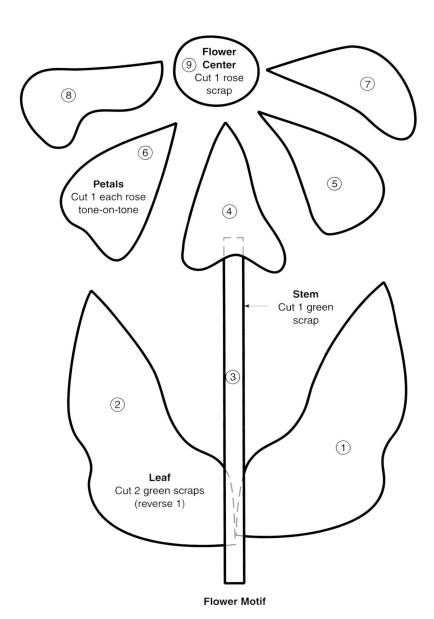

Flower Center
⑨ Cut 1 rose scrap

⑧

⑦

⑥

Petals
Cut 1 each rose tone-on-tone

④

⑤

Stem
Cut 1 green scrap

③

②

①

Leaf
Cut 2 green scraps (reverse 1)

Flower Motif

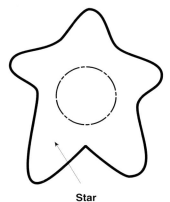

Star
Cut 1 each rose, green, navy & purple tone-on-tone

Floral Silhouettes
Templates
Actual Size

TUMBLING STRIPES THROW

Stitch this fast and fun quilt with the stripes tumbling horizontally and vertically.

Design | Carol Zentgraf

Project Specifications
Skill Level: Beginner
Quilt Size: 57" x 65½"

Materials
2 fat quarters each of six stripes
   for front
12 fat quarters of one or
   combination of stripes for back
½ yard striped fabric for
   binding
Batting 63" x 72"
Bias-tape maker

Cutting
From front stripes fat
   quarters, cut seven 9" squares
   from each of the six stripes
   for a total of 42 squares.

From back stripes fat quarters,
   cut (12) 18" squares.

From fabric for binding,
   cut 1⅞"-wide bias strips to
   total 7 yards when joined.

Completing the Quilt
Arrange front squares into seven horizontal rows of six squares each, placing one square of each fabric in each row. Alternate the direction of the stripes for each block and on alternating rows.

Sew squares together in each row. Press seam allowances to one side, alternating the direction on adjacent rows.

Sew the rows together, matching the corners of the squares. Press.

Sew back squares together in four rows of three squares each. Cut batting to fit the back.

Sandwich batting between back and front. Beginning in the centre and working toward the outside, pin layers together along seam lines and outer edges of the top. Stitch in the ditch along block seams to quilt. Trim batting and back even with edges of top.

Sew bias strips together. Trim seam allowances to ⅛" and press to one side. Follow bias-tape maker instructions to press strips into bias tape.

Open tape. On front of quilt, with raw edges even, sew narrow side of bias tape around edges, mitring corners.

Fold tape to back of quilt and pin in place. Stitch in the ditch on the front of the quilt, catching the edges of the binding on the back of the quilt to secure. ■

Tumbling Stripes Throw

GARDEN PATCH QUILT

Frayed edges form the petals in this garden of pastel posies.

Design | Sue Harvey

Project Specifications
Skill Level: Beginner
Quilt Size: 56" x 72"
Block Size: 8" x 8"
Number of Blocks: 18

Materials
17 pastel 1930s print fat quarters
3½ yards yellow print
Batting 60" x 76"
Backing 60" x 76"
All-purpose thread to match fabrics
Pastel-variegated machine-quilting thread
1 skein 6-strand yellow embroidery floss
Basting spray
Yo-yo template
Embroidery needle

Cutting
Cut four strips 8½" by fabric width yellow print; subcut into 17 squares 8½" x 8½" for flower background squares.

Cut two strips each 2½" x 44½", 2½" x 56½", 4½" x 56½" and 4½" x 64½" along remaining length of the yellow print; set aside for borders.

Cut 36 squares 4½" x 4½" yellow print for A.

From each pastel print fat quarter, cut two strips 2½" x 22" and one strip 2¼" x 22"; set aside the 2¼" strips for binding.

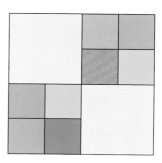

Four-Patch
8" x 8" Block
Make 18

Completing the Blocks
Join two randomly selected 2½" strips along length to make a strip set; repeat to make 17 strip sets. Cut each strip set into 2½" segments as shown in Figure 1.

Figure 1

Join two segments to make a Four-Patch unit as shown in Figure 2; repeat for 36 Four-Patch units. Set aside remaining segments for the pieced border.

Figure 2

Garden Patch Quilt

Sew an A square to one side of each Four-Patch unit as shown in Figure 3; press seams toward the Four-Patch unit.

Figure 3

Join two pieced strips to complete one Four-Patch block as shown in Figure 4; repeat for 18 blocks.

Figure 4

Trace one each 6½", 4½" and 2½" circles on one pastel print fat quarter using the purchased yo-yo template. *Note: If not using a purchased yo-yo template, make a template for each size circle.*

Cut out the circles to form flower shapes as shown in Figure 5; repeat with all pastel print fat quarters.

Figure 5   **Figure 6**

Lightly apply basting spray to the wrong side of a 6½" flower shape; centre it on a flower background square and smooth in place. Repeat to centre a 4½" flower shape and a 2½" flower shape on the larger flower shape as shown in Figure 6, using a different print for each size. Repeat to make 17 flower units.

Using pastel-variegated machine-quilting thread in the top of the machine and all-purpose thread in the bobbin, topstitch ½" inside the edge of each flower shape as shown in Figure 7.

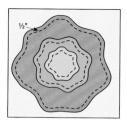

Figure 7

Completing the Quilt

Join two flower units with three Four-Patch blocks to make a row as shown in Figure 8; repeat for four rows.

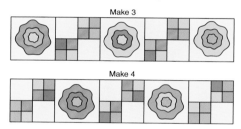

Figure 8

Join three flower units with two Four-Patch blocks to make a row, again referring to Figure 8; repeat for three rows.

Join the rows to complete the pieced centre, referring to the Placement Diagram for positioning of rows.

Sew the 2½" x 56½" yellow print border strips to opposite long sides of the pieced centre and the 2½" x 44½" yellow print border strips to the top and bottom; press seams toward strips.

For pieced border strip, join 15 of the 2½" segments (set aside earlier) as shown in Figure 9; repeat. Sew a strip to opposite long sides of the pieced centre.

Figure 9

Join 12 segments to make a border strip, again referring to Figure 9; repeat. Sew a strip to the top and bottom of the pieced centre.

Sew the 4½" x 64½" yellow print border strips to opposite long sides of the pieced centre and the 4½" x 56½" strips to the top and bottom to complete the top; press seams toward strips.

Prepare for quilting and quilt, referring to Getting Ready to Quilt (see page 14). *Note: The sample shown was professionally machine-quilted.*

Trim edges even. Join the 2¼" binding strips on short ends to make a long strip as shown in Figure 10. Press strip in half along length with wrong sides together; bind edges of quilt, referring to Finishing the Edges (see page 16).

Figure 10

Cut a 2½" circle from each pastel print fat quarter. Hand- or machine-baste ½" inside the edge of each circle using pastel-variegated machine-quilting thread; pull thread to draw edge tightly to the centre, knot thread and flatten to make a yo-yo, leaving the raw edge exposed at top of yo-yo as shown in Figure 11.

Figure 11

Use a 6" length of 6-strand yellow embroidery floss to attach a yo-yo to the centre of each flower, bringing the ends of the embroidery floss up through the centre of the yo-yo and knotting tightly; trim ends ⅛"–¼" beyond yo-yo.

Wash and dry quilt to fray edges of flowers. ■

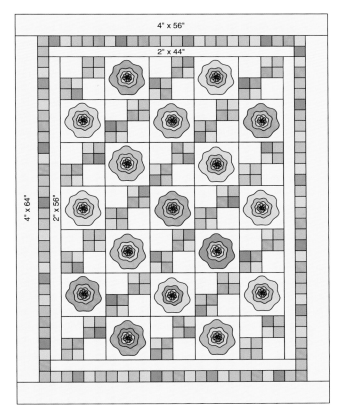

Garden Patch Quilt
Placement Diagram
56" x 72"

SUNNY DAYS

The yellow and gold fabrics used in this quilt remind us of summer.

Design | Julie Weaver

Project Specifications
Skill Level: Beginner
Quilt Size: 40" x 40"
Block Size: 12" x 12"
Number of Blocks: 4

Materials
4 fat quarters yellow or gold tone-on-tones or mottleds
½ yard yellow tone-on-tone
1 yard dark gold mottled
¾ yard yellow plaid
Batting 44" x 44"
Backing 44" x 44"
Yellow all-purpose thread
Brown/gold rayon twist thread

Completing the Blocks
Cut two 3½" x 22" strips each from the four yellow or gold fat quarters; subcut strips into 3½" square segments for A. You will need 12 A squares from each fabric.

Cut one 2½" x 22" strip dark gold mottled; subcut into 2½" square segments for B. You will need 16 B squares. Draw a diagonal line from corner to corner on the wrong side of each B square.

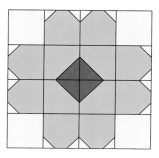

Sunny Days
12" x 12" Block
Make 4

Place a B square on an A square and stitch on marked line as shown in Figure 1; trim excess beyond the stitched line to ¼" to make one A-B unit, again referring to Figure 1. Repeat for all A squares to make 16 A-B units; set aside. Press B to the right side.

Figure 1

Cut two 3½"-by-fabric-width strips yellow tone-on-tone; subcut into 3½" square segments for C. You will need 16 C squares.

Sunny Days

Cut three 1½"-by-fabric-width strips yellow tone-on-tone; subcut into 1½" square segments for D. You will need 64 D squares. Draw a diagonal line from corner to corner on the wrong side of each D square.

Place a D square on one corner of an A square and stitch on marked line as shown in Figure 2; repeat on an adjacent corner. Trim excess ¼" beyond the stitched line and press D to the right side to complete one A-D unit, again referring to Figure 2; repeat for 8 A-D units of each fabric.

Figure 2

To piece one block, join two C squares with two same-fabric A-D units to make a row as shown in Figure 3; repeat for two rows. Press seams toward C.

Figure 3

Join two same-fabric A-D units with two same-fabric A-B units to make a row as shown in Figure 4; repeat for two rows. Press seams toward A-B units.

Figure 4

Join the A-D-C rows with the A-D-B rows to complete one block as shown in Figure 5; press seams in one direction. Repeat for four blocks.

Figure 5

Completing the Top

Cut two 2" x 22" strips from each of the four yellow or gold fat quarters. Arrange the strips as desired for colour order and sew together along length in that order; press seams in one direction.

Subcut the strip set into 1½" segments to make 1½" x 12½" E units as shown in Figure 6; you will need 12 E units.

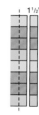

Figure 6

Cut one 12½"-by-fabric-width strip dark gold mottled; subcut into 1" segments for F. You will need 24 F segments.

Sew an F segment to opposite long sides of each E unit as shown in Figure 7; press seams toward E.

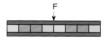

Figure 7

Join two blocks with three E-F units to make a block row as shown in Figure 8; repeat for two block rows. Press seams toward E-F units.

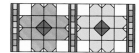

Figure 8

Cut nine 2½" x 2½" squares dark gold mottled for G.

Join two E-F units with three G squares to make a row as shown in Figure 9; repeat for three rows. Press seams toward G.

Figure 9

Join the E-F-G rows with the block rows to complete the pieced centre as shown in Figure 10; press seams toward E-F-G rows.

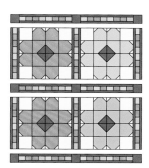

Figure 10

Cut two strips each 5½" x 30½" and 5½" x 40½" yellow plaid. Sew the shorter strips to opposite sides and longer strips to the top and bottom of the pieced centre; press seams toward strips.

Finishing the Quilt

Prepare for quilting and quilt as desired, referring to Getting Ready to Quilt (see page 14). *Note: The quilt shown was machine-quilted in the ditch of seams, ¼" from some seams, and then ½" from these seams using brown/gold rayon twist thread.*

Prepare 5 yards dark gold mottled binding and apply, referring to Finishing the Edges (see page 16) to finish. ■

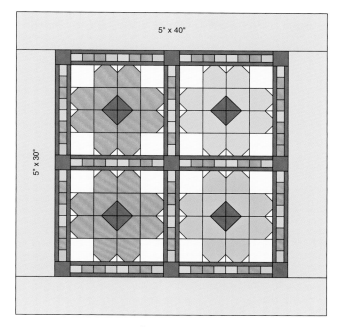

Sunny Days
Placement Diagram
40" x 40"

PRETTY MAIDS

Turn flower-colour fat quarters into a lap quilt of "pretty maids all in a row."

Design | Sue Harvey

Project Specifications
Skill Level: Beginner
Quilt Size: 56" x 68"
Block Size: 10" x 12"
Number of Blocks: 9

Materials
1 yellow print fat quarter
4 green print fat quarters
6 flower-colour print fat quarters
8 cream print fat quarters
1½ yards floral print
Backing 60" x 72"
Batting 60" x 72"
All-purpose thread to match fabrics

Completing the Blocks
Note: Fabrics are referred to as yellow, green, cream and flower throughout these instructions. All strips for this project are cut along the 22" length of the fat quarters.

Cut 26 strips 2½" x 22" from four cream fat quarters; subcut each strip into 2½" squares for A. You will need 204 A squares. Mark a diagonal line on the wrong side of each square.

From remaining cream fat quarters, cut the following: three strips 4⅞" x 22"—subcut into (12) 4⅞" squares for D; four strips 4½" x 22" for E; and six strips 4½" x 22"—subcut into four 2½" segments for F, eight 6½" segments for G, two 8½" segments for H and four 4½" squares for J.

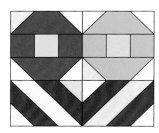

Pretty Maids
10" x 12" Block
Make 9

Cut two strips 4⅞" x 22" from each green fat quarter; subcut each strip into 4⅞" square segments for D. You will need 30 green D squares.

Place an A square on opposite corners of each green D square as shown in Figure 1.

Figure 1

Stitch on the marked diagonal line, trim seam allowance to ¼" and press A open as shown in Figure 2.

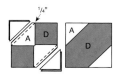

Figure 2

Pretty Maids

Cut the D square on the unstitched diagonal to make two A-D units as shown in Figure 3; repeat for 60 A-D units.

Figure 3

Place two cream E strips wrong sides together. Cut one end of the layered strips with a 45-degree angle as shown in Figure 4; subcut layered strips into 1⅞" segments to make E and ER segments, again referring to Figure 4. Repeat with remaining E strips to make nine each E and ER segments.

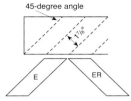

Figure 4

Cut six strips 2½" x 22" from one flower fat quarter; subcut into 12 segments 2½" x 6½" for B and 12 squares 2½" x 2½" for C. Repeat with each flower fat quarter.

Cut five yellow strips 2½" x 22"; subcut into 36 squares 2½" x 2½" for C.

To piece one flower unit, choose two B segments and two C squares of one flower colour. Place an A square on each end of B as shown in Figure 5; stitch on the marked diagonal line, trim seam allowance to ¼" and press A open. Repeat for two A-B units.

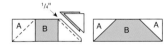

Figure 5

Sew a yellow C between the two flower C squares.

Sew the C strip between the A-B units to complete one flower unit as shown in Figure 6; repeat to make 36 flower units.

Figure 6

To piece one stem unit, sew an A-D unit to opposite sides of E as shown in Figure 7; repeat with ER.

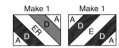

Figure 7

Join the pieced units to complete one stem unit as shown in Figure 8; repeat for nine stem units.

Figure 8

Join two flower units with one stem unit to complete one Pretty Maids block as shown in Figure 9; repeat for nine blocks.

Figure 9

Competing the Top

Join three blocks to make a row; repeat for three block rows.

Join six flower units to make a sashing row; repeat for three sashing rows.

Join the block rows with the sashing rows as shown in Figure 10.

Figure 10

Cut each cream D square on one diagonal to make triangles. Sew an A-D unit to each triangle to complete one leaf unit as shown in Figure 11; repeat for 24 leaf units.

Figure 11

Join six leaf units with two F, two G and one H segment to make a side strip as shown in Figure 12; repeat. Sew a strip to each side of the pieced centre, referring to the Placement Diagram for positioning of strips.

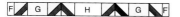

Figure 12

Join six leaf units with two G segments and two J squares to make an end strip as shown in Figure 13; repeat. Sew a strip to each end of the pieced centre Completing the Quilt referring to the Placement Diagram for positioning of strips.

Figure 13

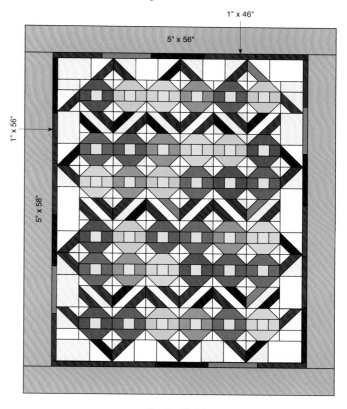

Pretty Maids
Placement Diagram
56" x 68"

Completing the Quilt

Cut four strips 1½" x 22" from each green fat quarter; cut each strip in half to make 11" lengths. Join strips randomly on short ends to make a long strip; press seams in one direction. Cut into two strips each 46½" long and 56½" long.

Sew the longer strips to opposite long sides of the pieced centre and the shorter strips to the ends; press seams toward strips.

Cut and piece two strips each 5½" x 56½" and 5½" x 58½" floral print. Sew the longer strips to opposite long sides of the pieced centre and the shorter strips to the ends; press seams toward strips.

Sandwich batting between the completed top and prepared backing piece; pin or baste to hold.

Hand- or machine-quilt as desired. *Note: The sample shown was professionally machine-quilted in an allover pattern.* Trim backing and batting even with the quilted top.

Cut seven strips floral print 2¼" by fabric width. Prepare and apply self-made binding referring, to Finishing the Edges (see page 16) to finish. ∎

WINDMILL TWIN QUILT

Pieced quilts are a great way to showcase the coordinating prints in a favourite fabric collection.

Design | Carol Zentgraf

Project Specifications
Skill Level: Beginner
Quilt Size: 75½" x 100½"

Materials
3 fat quarters each of 11 prints for quilt front
2 fat quarters each of 2 prints for quilt front
1½ yards each of 4 top prints for back
¾ yard of one top print for binding
Batting 82" x 107"
Bias-tape maker

Cutting
From quilt front print fat quarters, cut (16) 8" squares from each of 11 prints (total of 176 squares). Cut eight 8" squares from each of 2 prints (total of 16 squares). Subcut each 8" square in half diagonally and stack triangles according to fabric print.

From fabric for back, cut one 40" x 53" rectangle from each print for back.

From fabric for binding, cut 9½ yards of 1⅞"-wide bias for binding.

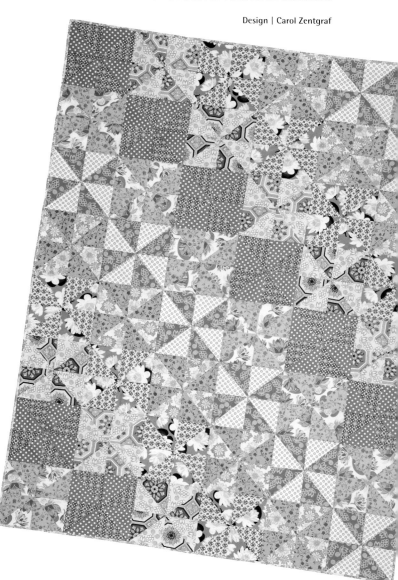

Completing the Quilt

Plan fabric placement for each windmill block, choosing two contrasting colours for each block. To assemble each block, sew contrasting triangles together in pairs along the long edges. Trim the block to 7" x 7". Sew four blocks together to create the windmill design (Figure 1). Press. Trim windmill block to 13" x 13". Repeat to assemble a total of 48 windmill blocks.

Figure 1

Arrange windmill blocks in eight horizontal rows of six blocks each. Sew blocks in each row together. Press seam allowances to one side, alternating direction on adjacent rows.

Sew the rows together, matching the corners of the squares. Press.

Sew long edges of two back rectangles together and press seams. Repeat with remaining two back rectangles. Sew joined rectangles together, matching seams, to make a 79½" x 104½" quilt back.

Cut batting to fit quilt back. Sandwich batting between back and front. Beginning in the centre and working toward the outside, pin layers together along seam lines and outer edges of the top. Stitch in the ditch along block seams to quilt. Trim batting and back even with edges of top.

Sew bias strips together. Trim seam allowances to ⅛" and press to one side. Follow bias-tape maker instructions to press strips into bias tape.

Open tape. On front of quilt, with raw edges even, sew narrow side of bias tape around edges, mitring corners.

Fold tape to back of quilt and pin in place. Stitch in the ditch on the front of the quilt, catching the edges of the binding on the back of the quilt to secure. ■

Windmill Twin Quilt

MAPLE LEAF RAGTIME

The autumn colours of maple leaves were the inspiration for this gorgeous classic scrap quilt.

Design | Willow Sirch

Project Specifications
Skill Level: Beginner
Quilt Size: 48" x 48"
Block Size: 8" x 8"
Number of Blocks: 20

Materials
20 different fat quarters in brick red, gold, orange and
  olive green tones
½ yard beige mottled for binding
1¼ yards muslin
Backing 52" x 52"
Batting 52" x 52"
All-purpose thread to match fabrics .
White hand-quilting thread

Notes
Fat quarters of Bali prints and other hand-printed cottons, along with a few small calico prints, were used to make the sample quilt. We recommend washing and ironing all fabrics before using in the quilt. Pay special attention to hand-dyed reds as these may require more than one washing to make colourfast.

Cutting
Cut one 2⅞" x 22" strip from each fat quarter; subcut into 2⅞" square segments. Cut each square in half on one diagonal to make A triangles; you will need 10 dark A triangles for each block, a total of 200 for the quilt.

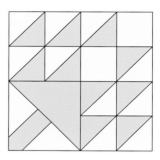

Maple Leaf
8" x 8" Block
Make 20

Cut one 4⅞" x 4⅞" square from each fat quarter; cut in half on one diagonal to make B triangles. Set aside one triangle of each fabric for another project.

Prepare template for E using pattern given; cut one E piece from each fat quarter.

Cut three 2½"-by-fabric-width strips muslin; subcut strips into 2½" square segments for C. You will need two C squares for each block, a total of 40 for the whole quilt.

Cut eight 2⅞"-by-fabric-width strips muslin; subcut strips into 2⅞" square segments. You will need 100 squares. Cut each square in half on one diagonal to make muslin A triangles; you will need 10 muslin A triangles for each block, a total of 200 for the whole quilt.

Maple Leaf Ragtime

Cut two 4⅜"-by-fabric-width strips muslin; subcut strips into 4⅜" square segments. You will need 10 squares. Cut each square on both diagonals to make D triangles as shown in Figure 1; you will need 40 D triangles.

Figure 1

Completing the Blocks

To piece one block, sew a muslin A to a coloured A to make a triangle/square unit as shown in Figure 2; repeat for 10 same-fabric A units. Press seams toward darker fabric.

Figure 2

Sew a muslin D to opposite sides of a same-fabric E as shown in Figure 3; press seams toward E.

Figure 3

Sew the D-E unit to B as shown in Figure 4; press seam toward B.

Figure 4

Join the pieced units, as shown in Figure 5, to make rows; join the rows to complete one Maple Leaf block. Press seams in one direction. Repeat for 20 blocks.

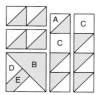

Figure 5

Completing the Quilt

Join four Maple Leaf blocks to make the pieced centre, referring to Figure 6; press seams in one direction.

Figure 6

Cut one strip 4½" x 22" from each fat quarter; subcut strips into 4½" square segments for F. You will need 64 F squares; set aside remaining squares for another project.

Join four different F squares to make a strip; press seams in one direction. Repeat for two strips. Sew a strip to opposite sides of the pieced centre as shown in Figure 7; press seams toward pieced strips.

Figure 7

Join six different F squares to make a strip; press seams in one direction. Repeat for two strips. Sew a strip to the top and bottom of the pieced centre, again referring to Figure 7; press seams toward pieced strips.

Join three blocks to make a strip as shown in Figure 8; repeat for a reverse strip, again referring to Figure 8. Sew the block strips to opposite sides of the pieced centre, referring to Figure 9; press seams toward F strips.

Figure 8

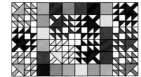

Figure 9

Join five blocks to make a strip as shown in Figure 10; repeat for a reverse strip, again referring to Figure 10. Sew the block strips to the top and bottom of the pieced centre, referring to Figure 11; press seams toward F strips.

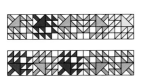

Figure 10

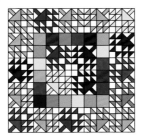

Figure 11

Join 10 F squares to make a strip; repeat for two strips. Sew to opposite sides of the pieced centre; press seams toward F strips. Join 12 F squares to make a strip; repeat for two strips. Sew to the top and bottom of the pieced centre to complete the pieced top; press seams toward F strips.

Prepare for quilting and quilt as desired, referring to Getting Ready to Quilt (see page 14). *Note: The project shown was hand-quilted ¼" from seams in the muslin pieces using white, hand-quilting thread.*

Prepare 6 yards beige mottled binding and apply, referring to Finishing the Edges (see page 16) to finish. ∎

Maple Leaf Ragtime
Placement Diagram
48" x 48"

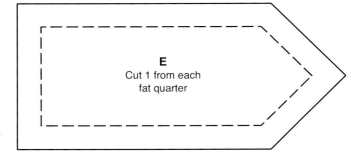

E
Cut 1 from each
fat quarter

Maple Leaf Ragtime
Template
Actual Size

WARM & COZY FLANNEL THROW

Quilt a pretty and practical flannel fat quarter quilt to keep you warm on cool winter nights.

Design | Chris Malone

Project Specifications

Skill Level: Beginner
Quilt Size: 39" x 39"

Materials

9 coordinating flannel fat quarters
2½ yards flannel
Batting 49 (5¼") squares
Soluble fabric glue stick
Freezer paper
Optional: walking foot

Notes

Prewash, dry and iron flannel. Preshrink batting if using cotton.

To use freezer paper as a cutting or sewing guide, draw the circle pattern onto the dull side of the paper and cut out. To use, press the shiny side onto fabric for about 3 seconds. Paper will hold while cutting or sewing, then can be peeled off and reused about five times.

Cutting

From fat quarters, cut a total of (49) 6½" squares for blocks. Cut (10) 4" circles from freezer paper and use to cut 25 circles from fat quarters.

From flannel yardage, cut (49) 6½" squares for backing blocks. Use freezer paper to cut 25 circles.

Completing the Throw

Arrange blocks in seven rows of seven blocks for the face of the quilt. Layer each fat-quarter circle with a flannel backing circle, both with right sides up.

Referring to the Placement Diagram (see page 98), place layered circles in centres of alternating blocks.

Centre a batting square on the wrong side of each backing block and adhere in place with a small amount of fabric glue stick.

Cut (10) 3" circles from freezer paper. Keeping the arranged order of rows, iron a circle of freezer paper to the centre of either the circle or the plain block. Pin this block to the layered backing block with wrong sides together. Sew around the edge of the circle using matching or contrasting thread. Peel off circle and repeat to complete all blocks in this manner.

Clip the seam allowance on each circle appliqué by making snips ¼"–⅜" apart perpendicular to the seam line, taking care not to clip into the stitching (Figure 1).

Figure 1

War and Peace

Warm & Cozy Flannel Throw

To assemble a row, pin blocks with back sides together and sew with a ½" seam allowance. Join rows in the same manner, matching seams.

Clip each seam, making snips perpendicular to seam line and ¼"–⅜" apart. To snip corners, make two diagonal cuts as shown in Figure 2.

Figure 2

To fray edges, wash throw in commercial washing machine and dry in dryer, checking occasionally for accumulated lint. Shake quilt outside when dry. ■

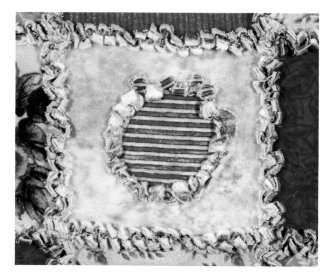

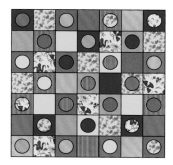

Warm & Cozy Flannel Throw
Placement Diagram
39" x 39"

PRETTY & PIECED

Four sweet gift bags can be made from the same six fat quarters by varying the placement of fabrics.

Designs | Connie Kauffman

Project Specifications

Skill Level: Easy
Gift Bag Size: Approximately 7¾" x 18½"

Materials for Two Bags

6 coordinating cotton fat quarters
1⅛ yards ¼"-wide ribbon

Simple Block Bag

Cutting

From one fat quarter, cut one 16½" x 11" rectangle for bottom portion of bag.

From one fat quarter, cut one 16½" x 8¾" rectangle for top portion of bag.

From each of the remaining four fat quarters, cut two 3¼" squares. Cut each square on each diagonal to make four triangles from each square (Figure 1).

Figure 1

From two of the four fat quarters, cut one 1" x 16½" strip from each.

Completing the Bag

Sew four different-colour triangles together to make eight blocks, using the same colour placement for each block (Figure 2).

Figure 2

Sew the blocks into a row; sew one 1" x 16½" strip on each side of the strip on each side of the pieced row to create a border (Figure 3).

Figure 3

Sew border to top and bottom sections (Figure 4).

Figure 4

Mark 5½" from top edge of bag and sew a small horizontal buttonhole for drawstring; cut open. Press top raw edge under ¼".

Fold bag right sides together and sew side and bottom edges. Finish edges with serger or zigzag stitches.

Turn top of bag to wrong side 2½"–2¾" and press. Stitch on inside folded edge and again approximately ¾" above that, making sure buttonhole is between the two sewn lines.

Turn bag right side out. Press. Cut ribbon in half. Thread one length through buttonhole and pull ends even. *Note: Set remaining length aside for Easy Gift Bag. At centre back of casing, stitch through ribbon to prevent it from pulling out.*

Easy Gift Bag

Instructions
Use two of the six fat quarters for top and bottom sections, and the remaining four fat quarters for pieced section.

Follow instructions for Simple Block Bag, except cut and piece the border as follows: From two fat quarters, cut one 1" x 16½" strip from each, from one fat quarter, cut six 2" x 2½" rectangles, and from one fat quarter, cut five 2" x 2½" rectangles.

Assemble rectangles alternately into a row, matching 2" sides. Trim excess fabric from row to fit. Sew strips to top and bottom of pieced row to create a border. ■

A STITCH IN TIME TOTE

Use fat quarters to sew an attractive tote bag that makes a great gift.

Design | Willow Ann Sirch

Project Specifications

Skill Level: Beginner

Tote Size: 16½" x 12" x 3½", excluding handles

Materials

1 fat quarter each of 8 prints in gold, orange and red (A–C and E–I) for checkerboard squares and Roman stripes

1 fat quarter white print (J) for triangles

3 fat quarters of 1 red print (D) for lining, handles and 2 diagonal strips

2 fat quarters of 1 orange print (K) for outer back, bottom and side gussets

Iron-on interfacing 12½" x 4½"

Quilter's square ruler

Cutting

For checkerboard squares, cut four 1½" x 22" strips each from A and B fat quarters.

For Roman stripes, cut two 1½" x 22" strips each from C, D and E–H fat quarters.

For triangle squares, cut two 3½" x 22" strips each from I and J fat quarters.

From D fat quarters, cut two 18" x 5" strips for handles, one 16½" x 4½" strip for lining bottom, two 12½" x 4½" strips for lining side gusset and one 16½" x 12½" rectangle for lining front and back.

From K fat quarters, cut one 16½" x 4½" strip for tote bottom, two 12½" x 4½" strips for outer side gusset, and one 16½" x 12½" rectangle for outer back.

Completing the Tote

With right sides together, sew short ends of two A strips together. Press seams to one side. Repeat with remaining two A strips. Join B strips in same manner. Sew A and B strips together alternately along long edges. Press seams in same direction.

Cutting across the seams, cut (16) 1½"-wide strips from the A/B unit. Sew four strips together in checkerboard pattern and trim into 4½" square (Figure 1). Repeat with remaining strips to make 4 checkerboard squares.

Figure 1

Match right sides of each pair of strips C, D, E, F, G and H, short ends together. Sew; press seams to one side. Sew strips together along one long side in the following order: C, D, E, F, G, H. Press seams in one direction.

A Stitch in Time Tote

Using a quilter's square ruler, cut four 4½" squares on the diagonal from pieced strips, aligning the middle of each square with the seam that runs through the middle of the 6-stripe pieced square. Press seams in one direction (Figure 2).

Figure 2

Match right sides of I strips together on short ends to make two long I strips. Repeat with the J strips. Sew I and J strips together along long edges. Using quilter's square ruler, cut eight triangles with a 6¼" base and 4½" sides, positioning triangles so they form two half-size triangles that meet along the middle seam. Sew triangles together along the base to make four squares. Press seams in one direction (Figure 3).

Figure 3

Following the Placement Diagram, arrange squares in sewing order. Sew squares together to make pieced front of tote. Press seams in one direction.

Centre and fuse interfacing to tote bottom strip. With right sides together, sew tote bottom along one side to bottom long side of pieced front. Press seams open. Sew opposite bottom edge to outer back bottom edge. Press seams open. Sew outer side gussets along sides and bottom to make outer tote. Follow same procedure to sew the tote lining.

With right sides together, sew lining to outer tote along top edge, leaving a 4" opening. Press seams open. Turn right side out through opening. Press lightly.

Press under short edges of handles ⅜". Fold long edges to the centre, and then fold handles in half along length. Topstitch around all edges. Topstitch ends of handles to front and back of tote approximately 6" from each side. ■

A Stitch in Time Tote
Placement Diagram
16½" x 12½"

APPLIQUÉD TOWEL TRIO

Embellished kitchen or bath hand towels are simple to sew, and make a great housewarming gift.

Designs | Phyllis Dobbs

Project Specifications

Skill Level: Beginner
Quilted Towel Size: 16½" x 26½"

Materials

One 16½" x 25½" dish towel each aqua, lime green
and black
1 fat quarter each aqua heart print, pink heart print,
multicoloured stripe and pink tonal
1⅛ yards pink medium rickrack
⅝ yard aqua medium rickrack
Fusible transfer web
20 aqua 6mm round faceted glass beads
8 green 6mm round faceted glass beads
2 aqua glass E beads
Beading needle

Cutting

For bottom trim on black towel, cut a 5½" x 18½"
rectangle from aqua heart print fat quarter. Prepare
templates for flower using pattern given.

For bottom trim on aqua towel, cut a 5½" x 18½"
rectangle from pink heart print fat quarter. Prepare
template for heart using pattern given.

For bottom trim on lime green towel, cut a 5½" x 18½"
rectangle from multicoloured stripe fat quarter.

Prepare templates for flower, heart and butterfly from
patterns given. Referring to Machine Appliqué (see
page 12), make a flower appliqué from pink heart print,
a heart appliqué and a butterfly body appliqué from pink
tonal, and butterfly wing appliqués from aqua heart print.

Cut two 18½" lengths of pink medium rickrack for black
and lime green towels. Cut one 18½" length of aqua
medium rickrack for aqua towel.

Completing the Towels

Sew a double ¼" hem on one long edge and both short edges of each bottom trim piece. Centre trim pieces on towels 4" above bottom edges of towels. Turn edges to back and pin in place. Stitch ⅛" from raw edge.

Pin rickrack over stitching, turning ends to back. Sew in place.

Referring to photo for placement, fuse appliqués to towels; machine-appliqué edges. Using the same stitch, sew two lines for butterfly antennae.

Sew an aqua E bead at the tip of each antenna. Sew three aqua faceted beads on heart and three at flower centre; randomly sew remaining aqua faceted beads to lime green and black towels. Sew green faceted beads randomly to aqua towel. ■

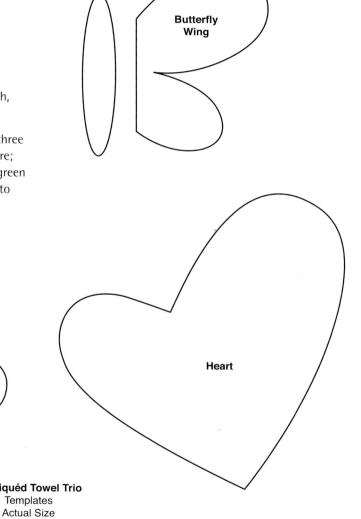

Butterfly Body

Butterfly Wing

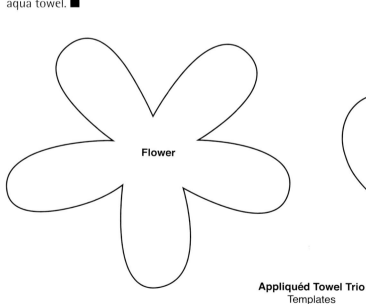

Flower

Heart

Appliquéd Towel Trio
Templates
Actual Size

Appliquéd Towel Trio

PATCHWORK BACKPACK

Quilt this perfect travel–size backpack. It's so easy to do, you'll want to make one for yourself and for a friend.

Design | Holly Daniels

Project Specifications
Skill Level: Easy
Backpack Size: Approximately 15" tall

Materials
8 fat quarters in light, medium and dark colours
Backing 16" x 44"
Lining 16" x 44", or 2 fat quarters
Thin quilt batting 16" x 40"
6 sets ⁷⁄₁₆" silver eyelets
Extra-large eyelet setter
Large snap or magnetic snap closure
Scraps fusible interfacing
Paper-backed fusible transfer web 4" x 4"
12 large-hole wooden beads
Tube turner or knitting needle

Cutting
Cut one 6½" square from one light fat quarter. Cut five 3½" squares from each light, medium and dark fat quarter for a total of (40) 3½" squares.

Cut one 3⅞" square from each fat quarter, plus four additional 3⅞" x 3⅞" squares from two of the darker fat quarters (12 total). Cut eight of the squares in half diagonally to make 16 triangles.

Cut two 2½" x 22" strips from one remaining fat quarter for straps.

Prepare template for bag bottom using pattern given. Cut one bag bottom each from a darker fat quarter, backing fabric, lining fabric and batting.

Cut and piece enough 2½"-wide strips from remaining fat quarters to equal 32" for binding.

Cut and piece enough 1½"-wide strips from remaining fat quarters to equal 22" for ties. *Note: If desired, substitute purchased cord.*

Cut one 15½" x 30½" rectangle each from backing fabric, lining fabric and batting.

Completing the Backpack
Place one 3⅞" dark-colour square into one corner of the 6½" square. Sew diagonally across smaller square. Trim away excess in seam allowance and press seam away from centre (Figure 1). Sew remaining three 3⅞" dark-colour squares to the remaining corners of 6½" square in same manner.

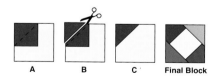

A   B   C   Final Block

Figure 1

Patchwork Backpack

Prepare heart template using pattern given. Referring to Machine Appliqué (see page 12), make one heart appliqué from medium or dark fat quarter. Fuse to centre of 6½" square. Machine-appliqué using blanket or satin stitch.

Sew triangles together in light/dark pairs (Figure 2). Press seams toward dark side. Sew two triangle units together with light fabrics toward centre. Repeat with two more triangle units. Sew two double triangle units together to form a square. Make a second square with remaining triangle units.

Make 8   Make 2 blocks

Figure 2

Referring to Placement Diagram, lay heart square and triangle squares on flat surface. Arrange 3½" squares as shown. *Note: Two squares will not be used.* Sew squares together in vertical rows. Press seams up in odd rows and down in even rows. Sew vertical strips together to form outer fabric.

Layer 15½" x 30½" rectangles of backing fabric, batting and outer fabric; pin or baste together. Using a variety of decorative machine stitches, stitch over seams to secure layers. Sew short sides of bag together to form a tube. Add decorative stitching over this seam as well.

Fold each strap in half lengthwise, right sides together, and sew to form long tubes. Turn right sides out. Press so seams are on centre backs.

Layer backing, batting and fat-quarter bag bottom pieces with batting in middle, and baste edges together. Mark front, back and ends of bag and of bottom with pins. With

right sides together, pin bag bottom to bag, matching at pins and pleating bag at rounded corners to fit.

Insert raw edges of straps two patches apart in seam. Sew bottom to bag. Pin opposite ends of straps to top edge of bag next to each other with raw edges even. Sew through straps and outer bag to hold in place.

Sew lining fabric and attach bottom in same manner as for bag. Place lining in bag, wrong sides together.

Measure 2" from centre top of bag and mark for placement of large snap or magnetic snap closure. Interface wrong side of lining at these points and attach snaps following manufacturer's instructions.

Sew binding strips together. Press seams. Fold strips in half lengthwise, wrong sides together, and press. Sew binding to right side of bag with raw edges even. Fold binding over raw edge and hand-stitch folded edge inside bag.

Follow manufacturer's instructions to attach six eyelets to each side of bag. Fold each strip for ties in half lengthwise, right sides together, and sew ½" from raw edge. Turn using a tube turner or knitting needle. Press. Thread ties through eyelets, draw up as desired and tie. Thread three wooden beads on each end of each tie; knot ends. Trim away excess fabric. ■

Patchwork Backpack
Placement Diagram
15½" x 30½"

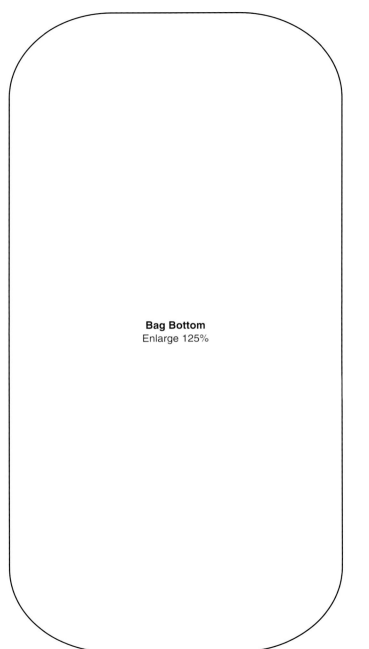

Bag Bottom
Enlarge 125%

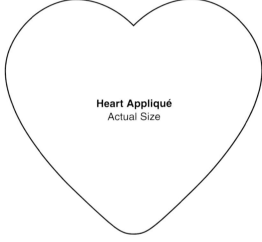

Heart Appliqué
Actual Size

Patchwork Backpack
Templates

SIT WITH ME & HAVE SOME TEA

This little, redwork quilt hanging from a rolling pin gives a cute look to any kitchen.

Design | Connie Kauffman

Project Specifications

Skill Level: Easy

Quilt Size: 13" x 19", including tabs

Materials

1 cotton fat quarter each red/black check, blue/black check, black cherries print, blue cherries print, white solid and black solid

3" x 6" scrap yellow cherries print

Batting 14" x 20"

13" red narrow rickrack

13" white medium rickrack

⅜ yard ⅜"-wide white lace

⅝ yard 1½"-wide red wire-edged ribbon

5 (½") red buttons

4 (⅜") white buttons

9 (⁵⁄₁₆") white buttons

Approximately 30 red seed beads

4½"–6½" diameter white crocheted doily

Miniature teaspoon

6-strand red embroidery floss

12" rolling pin

Seam sealant

Note

For quilt to hang properly on rolling pin, the barrel of the pin needs to be at least 9" long. If a 12" rolling pin cannot be found, a hanger for the quilt can be made by cutting a 1½" wooden dowel to desired size and gluing large wooden beads to the ends.

Cutting

From red/black check fat quarter, cut one 13½" x 2" strip for bottom, and two 1¾" x 5½" strips. Cut one 1¾" x 12½" strip; subcut into seven 1¾" squares.

From blue/black check fat quarter, cut one 2¼" x 13" strip.

From black cherries print fat quarter, cut one 13½" x 2¾" strip for bottom.

From blue cherries print fat quarter, cut two 1¾" x 4¼" strips. Cut one 1¾" x 12½" strip; subcut into seven 1¾" squares.

From white solid fat quarter, cut one 8" x 8" block for teapot embroidery, one 1¾" x 5½" A strip, and one 6¾" x 1¾" B strip.

From black solid fat quarter, cut two 1¾" x 16" strips; subcut into (17) 1¾" squares. Cut one 13½" x 16¾" rectangle for backing, and two 4" x 8" rectangles for hanging tabs.

Completing the Quilt

Transfer embroidery template onto 8" x 8" white block. Using 2 strands red embroidery floss and outline stitch (see stitch illustration), embroider transferred lines.

Outline Stitch

Cut doily in half. Immediately apply seam sealant; let dry. Sew cut edge of doily under straight embroidered line using a small zigzag stitch.

Lay out blocks and strips as shown in Figure 1 and sew into rows. Sew rows together to make two units (top and bottom); sew units together. Sew the 2¼" x 13" blue/black check strip to the right side of the unit.

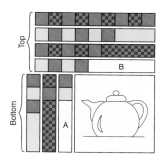

Figure 1

Sew red rickrack on blue/black check strip ¼" from seam line. Sew white rickrack ¼" from red rickrack. Trim ends of rickrack even with ends of strip.

Place the red/black check and the black cherries bottom strips with right sides together. Sandwich 13" length of lace between strips along one long edge. Sew strips together using a ¼" seam, catching edge of lace in seam (Figure 2). Trim ends of lace even with fabric strips. Press seam open and press lace over black cherries strip.

Figure 2

Fold yellow cherries squares diagonally twice to make triangle prairie points (Figure 3). Position the first triangle point 1½" from the edge of the red/black check strip. Position the second triangle beside the first, overlapping it ¼" Hand-stitch the points to the red/black check strip with raw edges even.

Figure 3

Sew the red/black check strip to the bottom of the pieced unit. *Note: Take care not to catch doily in stitching. Press strips down.*

Fold the black 4" x 8" rectangles for hanging tabs in half lengthwise (2" x 8") and sew long edges together. Turn right side out. Press with seams in centres of tab strips.

Place pieced top and backing, right sides together, on top of batting. Pin layers together. Position tabs 1½" in from each side on the wrong side of the quilt front. *Note: If needed, space tab position to hang over dowel or rolling pin before sewing.* Sew around edges, leaving a 3" opening at bottom for turning. Trim seams and clip corners. Turn right side out. Turn opening edges under and hand-stitch closed. Press.

Quilt as desired by stitching in the ditch along pieced strips, and around embroidered teapot. Randomly sew red seed beads to white background with black thread, knotting each bead on back of quilt.

Beginning at left-hand side of quilt, sew one white button in lower left corner of each red/black check strip or square across the quilt. Sew the four remaining white buttons across the red/black check bottom strip on the right-hand side of the quilt. Sew red buttons evenly spaced down the right-hand side of the blue/black check strip.

Tie wire-edged ribbon in a bow around the teaspoon and stitch securely in place over the triangles. ■

Sit With Me & Have Some Tea
Embroidery Template
Actual Size

PRETTY & PINK

Book-jacket covers are great gifts for readers, but be sure to make one for your journal, your calendar and your personal reading.

Design | Julie Higgins

Project Specifications

Skill Level: Beginner
Book-Jacket Cover Size: 5" x 7½", closed;
    10" x 7½", opened

Materials

3 coordinating fat quarters
3 (8" x 10½") pieces fusible interfacing
Optional: 1 (10" x 12") piece fusible batting*
10" (½"-wide) ribbon for each cover
Optional embellishments: lace, beads, appliqué, etc.
*Substitute this for one of the pieces of fusible interfacing if quilting one of the covers.

Cutting

Note: To speed production, stack fat quarters and cut at one time as shown in Cutting Diagram; and then mix and match pieces when assembling. Lay out and label pieces for each book-jacket cover. Work only one cover at a time until familiar with the assembly process.

From coordinating fat quarters, cut one 8" x 10½" rectangle for outside cover (A). *Important: If quilting any of the covers, cut that outside cover 10" x 12".* Cut two 8" x 3" rectangles for inside covers (B), two 4" x 8" rectangles for contrast trim (C) and one 8" x 7" rectangle for inside lining (D). *Optional: Cut two 10" x 2" strips for each set of handles desired (E).*

Option: If quilting outside cover, fuse batting to wrong side of cover and quilt as desired; trim cover to 8" x 10½".

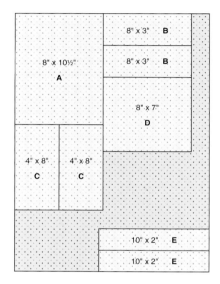

Pretty & Pink
Cutting Diagram

Completing the Quilt

With right sides together, matching 8" raw edges on one side, sew one B piece to one C piece. Fold so right sides are out and the remaining 8" edges are even. Press. *Note: When pressed, the larger contrast trim piece C will extend approximately ⅜" on the top edge of the pocket, creating the trim.* Repeat with remaining B and C pieces to form the lined pockets into which the covers of the book will be inserted on the jacket.

Place A piece right side up. If using handles, fold E strips in half lengthwise with right sides together. Sew together. Turn right sides out and press. Place handles on outside cover with raw edges even and pin in place. Place ribbon length just to left or right of the centre of A piece (as you are looking at it) for bookmark (Figure 1).

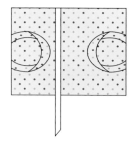

Figure 1

Place B/C units face down on A piece with raw edges even and trimmed edge face down.

Finish both 8" edges of D piece using serger or zigzag stitches. Layer D piece face down over A and B/C pieces, centring D piece horizontally with top and bottom raw edges even. *Note: Pull bottom end of ribbon bookmark up inside cover to avoid catching ribbon in seam.* Pin layers together around outer edges.

Sew around outside edge of layered pieces through all thicknesses, catching raw edges of B/C units, ends of handles and one end of ribbon bookmark in stitching. Clip corners. Turn right side out. Press. Embellish as desired. ■

LITTLE SCRAPPY PINCUSHIONS

These fun little pincushions are a great way to use scraps from your other fat quarter projects.

Designs | Carol Zentgraf

Project Specifications

Skill Level: Beginner

Large Strawberry Size: Approximately 6" in circumference (at top) x 3" tall

Medium Strawberry Size: Approximately 5½" in circumference (at top) x 2½" tall

Tomato Size: Approximately 10" in circumference x 1½" tall

Pyramid Size: Approximately 3½" x 3" x 3½"

Pieced Square Size: Approximately 3½" x 3½"

Materials

Scraps assorted-print fat quarters

Scraps wool felt

Assorted buttons

Lightweight cord or narrow ribbon

Cotton stuffing

Permanent fabric adhesive

Note

Buttons are stitched on by hand using a doubled thread.

Strawberry

Instructions

Prepare template for strawberry pincushion and strawberry cap using patterns given. Cut one strawberry piece from fat quarter scrap and one strawberry cap from wool felt scrap.

Sew straight edges of strawberry piece together to make a cone. Turn right side out and press the seam. Stuff firmly with cotton stuffing to the top of the strawberry.

Using a hand-sewing needle and a double thread, run a gathering stitch around the upper edge of the strawberry. Pull thread to tightly gather the upper edge and knot thread ends to secure.

Sew a button to the centre of the felt strawberry cap. Glue the cap to the top of the strawberry over gathers.

Tomato

Instructions

Prepare templates for tomato panel and tomato cap using patterns given. Cut eight tomato panels from fat quarter scraps and one tomato cap from wool felt scrap.

Sew panels together, leaving ½" unstitched at one end. Turn right side out and press. Stuff firmly with cotton stuffing; slipstitch open end closed.

Wrap cord around pincushion eight times, covering seams and twisting cords around each other at centre top and bottom. Secure to centre top and bottom with small dots of permanent fabric adhesive.

Glue tomato cap to top of pincushion. Centre a button on cap and hand-sew in place, stitching up from bottom of pincushion, through buttonholes and back down, repeating for a four-hole button. Pull thread to indent top and knot thread ends securely on bottom.

Pyramid

Instructions

Prepare templates for triangle and flower using patterns given. Cut four triangles and one 4" square from fat quarter scraps and two flowers from wool felt scraps.

Sew sides of triangles together. Sew square to bottoms of triangles, leaving an opening for turning. Turn right side out. Press. Stuff firmly with cotton stuffing.

Slipstitch opening closed. Edgestitch around base of pyramid.

Centre flowers with buttons in centres on opposite sides of pincushion. Stitch in place through button centres, stitching back and forth between the two sides and pulling the thread to indent. Knot thread securely under one flower.

Pieced Square

Instructions

Cut four 2¼" squares and one 4" square from fat quarter scraps. Cut one flower from wool felt scrap.

Referring to photo, sew 2¼" squares together and press the seams. Sew pieced squares to the 4" square, right sides together, leaving an opening for turning. Turn right side out. Press. Stuff firmly with cotton stuffing. Slipstitch opening closed.

Wrap cord around pincushion, covering seams. Knot cord ends together at centre top. Centre a flower with a button centre on top of pincushion. Stitch in place through the button, stitching all the way through the pincushion and back through the top, pulling the thread to indent. *Note: Stitch over cord at centre bottom of pincushion to tack in place.* Knot thread under flower to secure. ∎

Little Scrappy Pincushions

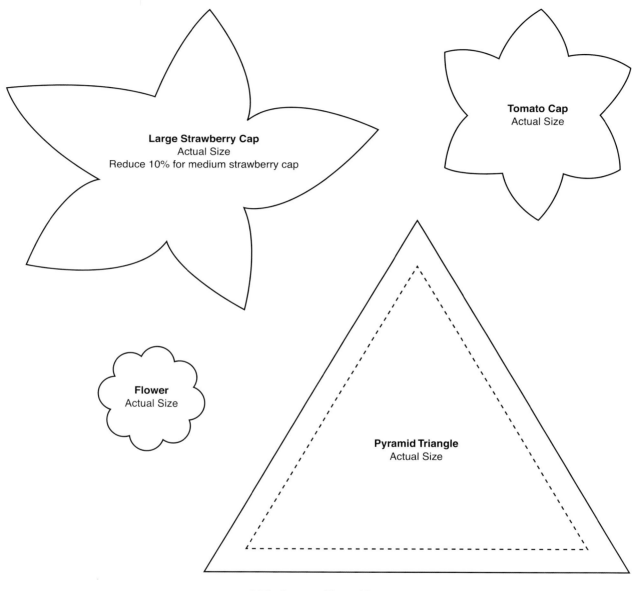

Large Strawberry Cap
Actual Size
Reduce 10% for medium strawberry cap

Tomato Cap
Actual Size

Flower
Actual Size

Pyramid Triangle
Actual Size

Little Scrappy Pincushions
Templates

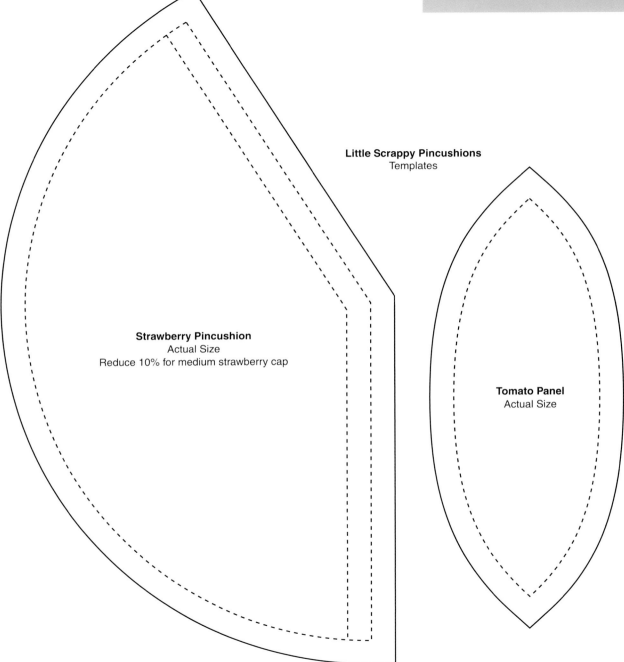

Little Scrappy Pincushions
Templates

Strawberry Pincushion
Actual Size
Reduce 10% for medium strawberry cap

Tomato Panel
Actual Size

INDEX

Welcoming Baby

Hugs & Kisses Baby Blanket, 18

Sweet Baby Quilt, 22

Baby Block Play Mat, 25

Baby Blocks With Love, 28

Stitched With Love Quilt & Tote, 32

Baby Bibs Twins, 38

Down on the Farm Gift Set, 44

Dress Your Table

Summer Delight Runner, 49

Pink & Green Squared, 52

Sunflower Sensation, 56

Cherry Pickin', 59

Posy Cozy & Coasters, 64

Floral Silhouettes, 69

INDEX

Simple Throws & Quilts

Tumbling Stripes Throw, 74

Garden Patch Quilt, 76

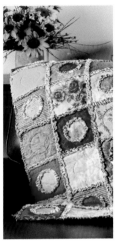

Sunny Days, 80

Pretty Maids, 84

Windmill Twin Quilt, 89

Maple Leaf Ragtime, 92

Warm & Cozy Flannel Throw, 96

Quick-to-Stitch Surprises

Pretty & Pieced, 99

A Stitch in Time Tote, 102

Appliquéd Towel Trio, 105

Patchwork Backpack, 108

Sit With Me & Have Some Tea, 112

Pretty & Pink, 116

Little Scrappy Pincushions, 119

Metric Conversion Charts

Metric Conversions

yards	x	.9144	=	metres (m)
yards	x	91.44	=	centimetres (cm)
inches	x	2.54	=	centimetres (cm)
inches	x	25.40	=	millimetres (mm)
inches	x	.0254	=	metres (m)

centimetres	x	.3937	=	inches
metres	x	1.0936	=	yards

Standard Equivalents

⅛ inch	=	3.20 mm	=	0.32 cm
¼ inch	=	6.35 mm	=	0.635 cm
⅜ inch	=	9.50 mm	=	0.95 cm
½ inch	=	12.70 mm	=	1.27 cm
⅝ inch	=	15.90 mm	=	1.59 cm
¾ inch	=	19.10 mm	=	1.91 cm
⅞ inch	=	22.20 mm	=	2.22 cm
1 inch	=	25.40 mm	=	2.54 cm
⅛ yard	=	11.43 cm	=	0.11 m
¼ yard	=	22.86 cm	=	0.23 m
⅜ yard	=	34.29 cm	=	0.34 m
½ yard	=	45.72 cm	=	0.46 m
⅝ yard	=	57.15 cm	=	0.57 m
¾ yard	=	68.58 cm	=	0.69 m
⅞ yard	=	80.00 cm	=	0.80 m
1 yard	=	91.44 cm	=	0.91 m

1⅛ yard	=	102.87 cm	=	1.03 m
1¼ yard	=	114.30 cm	=	1.14 m
1⅜ yard	=	125.73 cm	=	1.26 m
1½ yard	=	137.16 cm	=	1.37 m
1⅝ yard	=	148.59 cm	=	1.49 m
1¾ yard	=	160.02 cm	=	1.60 m
1⅞ yard	=	171.44 cm	=	1.71 m
2 yards	=	182.88 cm	=	1.83 m
2⅛ yards	=	194.31 cm	=	1.94 m
2¼ yards	=	205.74 cm	=	2.06 m
2⅜ yards	=	217.17 cm	=	2.17 m
2½ yards	=	228.60 cm	=	2.29 m
2⅝ yards	=	240.03 cm	=	2.40 m
2¾ yards	=	251.46 cm	=	2.51 m
2⅞ yards	=	262.88 cm	=	2.63 m
3 yards	=	274.32 cm	=	2.74 m
3⅛ yards	=	285.75 cm	=	2.86 m
3¼ yards	=	297.18 cm	=	2.97 m
3⅜ yards	=	308.61 cm	=	3.09 m
3½ yards	=	320.04 cm	=	3.20 m
3⅝ yards	=	331.47 cm	=	3.31 m
3¾ yards	=	342.90 cm	=	3.43 m
3⅞ yards	=	354.32 cm	=	3.54 m
4 yards	=	365.76 cm	=	3.66 m
4⅛ yards	=	377.19 cm	=	3.77 m
4¼ yards	=	388.62 cm	=	3.89 m
4⅜ yards	=	400.05 cm	=	4.00 m
4½ yards	=	411.48 cm	=	4.11 m
4⅝ yards	=	422.91 cm	=	4.23 m
4¾ yards	=	434.34 cm	=	4.34 m
4⅞ yards	=	445.76 cm	=	4.46 m
5 yards	=	457.20 cm	=	4.57 m

FEELING CRAFTY? GET CREATIVE!

Each 160-page book features easy-to-follow, step-by-step instructions and full-page colour photographs of every project. Whatever your crafting fancy, there's a Company's Coming Creative Series craft book to match!

Beading: Beautiful Accessories in Under an Hour

Complement your wardrobe, give your home extra flair or add an extra-special personal touch to gifts with these quick and easy beading projects. Create any one of these special crafts in an hour or less.

Knitting: Easy Fun for Everyone

Take a couple of needles and some yarn and see what beautiful things you can make! Learn how to make fashionable sweaters, comfy knitted blankets, scarves, bags and other knitted crafts with these easy-to-intermediate knitting patterns.

Card Making: Handmade Greetings for All Occasions

Making your own cards is a fun, creative and inexpensive way of letting someone know you care. Stamp, emboss, quill or layer designs in a creative and unique card with your own personal message for friends or family.

Patchwork Quilting

In this book full of throws, baby quilts, table toppers, wall hangings—and more—you'll find plenty of beautiful projects to try. With the modern fabrics available, and the many practical and decorative applications, patchwork quilting is not just for Grandma!

Crocheting: Easy Blankets, Throws & Wraps

Find projects perfect for decorating your home, for looking great while staying warm or for giving that one-of-a-kind gift. A range of simple but stunning designs make crocheting quick, easy and entertaining.

Sewing: Fun Weekend Projects

Find a wide assortment of easy and attractive projects to help you create practical storage solutions, decorations for any room or just the right gift for that someone special. Create table runners, placemats, baby quilts, pillows and more!

For a complete listing of Company's Coming cookbooks and craft books, check out

www.companyscoming.com